Maximizing Profit

Maximizing Profit
How to Measure the
Financial Impact of
Manufacturing Decisions

Walt Thrun

Productivity Press · New York

Most Productivity Press books are available at quantity discounts when purchased in bulk. For more information contact our Customer Service Department (800-394-6868). Address all other inquiries to:

Productivity Press
444 Park Avenue South, Suite 604
New York, NY 10016
United States of America
Telephone: 212-686-5900
Fax: 212-686-5411
E-mail: info@productivityinc.com

Cover design by Design Plus
Page design and composition by William H. Brunson, Typography Services
Printed and bound by Malloy Lithographic in the United States of America

Library of Congress Cataloging-in-Publication Data

Thrun, Walt.
    Maximizing profit : how to measure the financial impact of manufacturing decisions / Walt Thrun.
       p.   cm.
    Includes bibliographical references and index.
    ISBN 1-56327-271-7
    1. Corporate profits.   2. Rate of return.   I. Title.
HG4028.P7 T487 2002
658.15'5—dc21

                                        2002014878

06 05 04 03 02   10 9 8 7 6 5 4 3 2 1

Dedication

To the source and giver of all wisdom and understanding;
to the giver and sustainer of life itself.
Thank you Jesus

To my life's partner, Patt.
To our children and extended family:
Wally (aka) Reuben, Jim, Stephanie, Lori, Tracy,
Rebecca, Benjamin, and baby Emily.

David Brown, a teacher of teachers, who introduced me
to the wonderful world of mathematics and
physical sciences and has inspired over 10,000
others in the fulfillment of his calling.

CONTENTS

ACKNOWLEDGMENTS

A project such as this is only possible with the contribution and support of countless others including:

Wally and Jim Thrun, who provided wise and patient counsel especially relative to software issues.

H. Lee Beard and H. David Paris, who provided invaluable and comprehensive reviews of the original manuscript.

Mike Pierce, who, as a plant manager, was the first to apply the concepts in total into his plant operations.

Dr. Tom Carment, who was the first academician to espouse the concepts in total.

Rob Renfro, who as a Design Engineer for Gear Products, Inc. was a leader in converting from the OpTek Algorithm to the use of Excel optimization software.

Melinda Knight, who, as the owner and operator of Dot's Café in Claremore, Oklahoma, served Patt and myself a daily helping of ham, eggs, and humor during the completion stages of this project.

Of course, Maura May, Emily Pillars, and Bob Cooper of Productivity Press were always professional in the acquisition and development of this project.

FOREWORD

In a seamless presentation, this book brings together the concepts of the theory of constraints, systems thinking, and the application of constrained optimization to address how to make strategic manufacturing decisions that are optimal relative to financial performance. The result is a "must read" book for all practitioners and students of manufacturing.

The author skillfully integrates two difficult subjects, i.e., the theory of constraints and pro-forma financial measures. He accomplishes this by telling the story of a team of managers who consider and recommend manufacturing decisions. The OpTek management team members are asked by the general manager to put aside their prior assumptions and follow the financial impact of using the theory of constraints and optimization techniques to assist in their decisions. By presenting concepts with their applications, this book illustrates how the reader can make decisions that will increase cash flow for his or her business. It provides a framework that enhances decision making—one that deals with time, contribution margin, and opportunity costs.

As a teacher of *management accounting* I know that existing financial performance measurement systems are inadequate for those in the industrial sector. Granted, management accounting has progressed significantly since the days of traditional cost accounting, but there are still many conflicting theories. For example, we are still obsessed with assigning all factory costs to products and pursuing ever higher total plant utilization rates. This book illustrates the fallacy and dangers of such traditional practices.

The best that standard cost accounting can teach is "not to follow counterproductive practices" through cost minimization. The following is an analogy to changing behavior patterns. "If you want to counter certain behavior, you provide punishment. If you want to encourage certain behavior, you must provide rewards." Cost allocations are analogous to punishment. The decision maker will learn to make decisions to minimize the cost driver. Maximizing the proforma financial measure in manufacturing planning, through the concept of optimization techniques, is analogous to providing a reward. Through considering the financial impact, the decision maker will learn to make decisions to maximize the potential contribution margin.

By using the Excel Solver module to execute the OpTek Algorithm (Appendix B, pp. 193–204), the reader can investigate the concept of optimization techniques, simply by "virtually" following along with the text and entering new data as the decisions are presented chapter by chapter. Readers of this text will learn complex material more effectively than with traditional texts, because of the interactive format.

I have addressed, as a consultant and employee, problems with time, contribution margin, and opportunity costs in manufacturing firms that would have been avoided by understanding and applying the concepts of optimization techniques explained in this book. The following are but a few of the problems I have encountered, which would have been avoided if optimization techniques had been applied. A widespread problem in manufacturing is myopia—setting a goal and pursuing it without considering time. Failure to consider contribution margin is also commonly the source of problems. Finally, opportunity costs are important elements of the investment decision that are often ignored or handled implicitly. The OpTek Algorithm provides them explicitly and uses them correctly to identify potential capital budget investments.

I was a financial analyst for Ford Motor Company and CONOCO, Inc. for a combined period of eight years and was also in marketing at Burroughs Corporation. I have taught both undergraduate cost and graduate managerial accounting at Northeastern State University for the past 20 years. Additionally, I have published a teaching case on manufacturing accounting. I am a member of the IMA, AICPA, and Managerial Accounting Section of AAA.

Maximizing Profit is *not* just another textbook that is "boring with lots of calculations." It is both interesting and easy to read. It is recommended to business managers and college students desiring to understand the integration of production decisions and accounting.

Thomas M. Carment, Ph.D., CPA
Professor of Accounting and Department Chair, Accounting and Finance
Northeastern State University
Tahlequah, OK

PREFACE

Product and process technology has made tremendous strides in recent years, but progress in developing meaningful financial measures for manufacturers has sadly not kept pace.

This book introduces techniques that allow managers to measure the financial effects of manufacturing, and understand in advance which activities will maximize plant profitability. These techniques are used in this book in a way that makes them easy to understand and apply.

The material for this book was developed over two decades of working as both plant controller and manufacturing manager for three blue chip firms. I learned the concepts in graduate school while at California State University at Fullerton. Armed with these concepts and an industrial engineering background, I was very anxious to put these ideas into practice.

My original article introducing this thinking was published in *Management Accounting* nearly three decades ago. That article won a national certificate of recognition and was the beginning of efforts to develop and employ contemporary financial measures for manufacturers, thereby making manufacturers more effective and profitable. Since that time, the material or portions thereof have been published in several other publications, including *Modern Casting*, *The Management of Production*, and *Contemporary Cost Accounting*. The material has also been presented at national conferences of the Production/Operations Management Society and the Southern Management Association, as well as to regional chapters of the APICS, the Society of Manufacturing Engineers, the American Institute of Industrial Engineers, the American Society for Quality, and the Oklahoma Alliance for Manufacturing Excellence. The material has been enthusiastically endorsed by proponents of lean manufacturing, as well as the Institute of Management Accountants.

Today I am still one of a limited number in academia that has a passion for manufacturing excellence and a sincere desire for the continued success of America's industrial sector. When I was encouraged to write this latest version it was suggested that it be brief, succinct, and reader friendly. I trust that this text will be exactly that.

Walt Thrun
Assistant Professor of Business and Industry

INTRODUCTION

Measures have been developed in the past based on traditional standard cost concepts, in an attempt to predict and track the results of a given manufacturing action, but these measures have not proven effective. Standard cost concepts attempt to measure the financial impact of manufacturing actions based solely on cost reduction or cost avoidance. This book establishes techniques allowing the economic effects of manufacturing decisions to be determined, revealing which decisions will be the most profitable.

These techniques are based on concepts of "optimization technology," and in fact to be more specific, "constrained optimization." Such concepts are really quite basic. Consider that a part—a gear blank—sells for $10 each. The variable cost to make each gear blank is $6. Therefore, the contribution (that amount of the selling price that contributes to covering fixed cost and generate profit) is $4, i.e., selling price $10 minus variable cost $6 = $4. Then if ten gear blanks are made and sold in a given time period they would generate total revenue of $100, total variable cost of $60 and total contribution of $40. Consider further that the manufacturing process for the gear blank consists of one step that requires .5 hours per gear blank and the equipment can be operated for 180 hours per month. With this scenario, if the equipment was fully utilized to make gear blanks there would be 360 gear blanks made and sold during the month, generating total revenue of $3,600, total variable cost of $2,160, and total contribution of $1,440. Optimization techniques will allow this basic logic to be employed when multiple products with multiple processing steps with multiple equipment are considered simultaneously to achieve a stated objective. The objective may range from maximizing revenue to maximizing equipment utilization. The challenge is to determine which objective ultimately generates the most total profit. These concepts are valuable to manufacturers for two primary reasons:

1. Existing traditional financial measures provide misleading results because they do not address total plant performance, that is, they focus on local optimization.

2. Existing traditional financial measures do not have simulation capabilities because, as mentioned above, they do not encompass the financial aspects of manufacturing decisions holistically.

During our process of creating a more effective and profitable business, we need to begin by identifying just exactly what it is we are trying to accomplish in our plants. The concepts of "lean" manufacturing have been very popular in recent years, and justifiably so as they prove effective both in theory and, more importantly, in practice. It needs to be asked, however, do all lean operational activities result in an improvement in a plant's bottom line? Does "value added" equate with "profit improvement"?

Lean improvements, as currently practiced, typically address the aspect of waste associated with shopfloor production activities. However, the waste associated with using traditional performance measures based on the standard cost system far exceeds the waste identified through current lean or just-in-time (JIT) manufacturing practices.

Let's say, for example, that a plant is managed with a standard cost system where total plant utilization is a primary goal. Plant utilization is a common goal because fixed overhead traditionally is absorbed (the process of transferring manufacturing expenses to the balance sheet in the form of a current asset called *work-in-process inventory*) relative to the degree of plant utilization. This is just an accounting practice that defers expenses to another time period similar to what WorldCom recently did that got them into so much hot water. The point is, however, that the product mix that absorbs the most overhead may generate only half of the profit that the plant is capable of generating with a product mix that absorbs only half of the overhead. This is due to the fact there is no relationship between overhead absorption and total plant profitability. The amount of profit that the plant could generate minus the amount of profit generated while blindly pursuing the goal of total overhead absorption is correctly termed "waste." This is just one of the "**seven deadly sins of manufacturing**" that generates tremendous amounts of waste, i.e., profits foregone due to pursuing localized goals not related to total plant profitability. All seven of the deadly sins will be illustrated in detail in this text.

Lean improvements have also been primarily localized in scope, but the focused pursuit of any single manufacturing activity in isolation may be financially detrimental to the total plant's financial well-being. In addition, lean improvements have been primarily tactical in nature and focused on execution. Improving the efficiency of existing efforts assumes that our plants are already strategically pursuing the most relevant, effective, and productive activities, or "doing the right things" and trying to do them better. But, what if our plants are doing the "wrong things"? Making these activities more efficient will not make our company more effective.

On the other hand, as we work to improve our plants, will current financial measures accurately reflect the benefits associated with lean manufacturing? Consider a situation in which a plant has just journeyed through extensive training in lean manufacturing concepts, yet still pursues plant utilization as one of its primary performance goals. Current thinking allows that any operational "improvement" should automatically translate into financial improvement. However, if a plant evaluates operating improvements using misleading performance measures such as plant utilization, then the financial benefit of such operating improvement is misstated at best and negated at worst.

Many have said that the standard cost system must go, but what alternatives are offered? We sorely need relevant financial measures that will enable us to identify and eliminate the type of waste associated with employing outdated, counterproductive, and ineffective practices as we continue to sharpen our execution skills.

This book provides an alternative approach for measuring the financial impact of manufacturing choices, including activities associated with lean manufacturing. Using numerous illustrations of applications in a real plant environment, the text explains how counterproductive practices can be eliminated and total plant performance can be made more effective.

Chapters 2 and 3 expose the inherent weaknesses of current traditional thinking, and the following thirteen chapters introduce alternatives. Chapter 4 identifies and illustrates an effective plant performance measure using optimization techniques. Chapters 5 through 8 apply this technique to such common manufacturing choices as the make-or-buy decision, the subcontracting decision, evaluating potential new work, and more. Chapters 9 and 10 apply optimization techniques to the capital budgeting decision. Chapters 11 through 14 illustrate application to the aggregate planning process, while Chapter 15 focuses on multiple plant operations.

The CD included with this book will allow the reader to be virtually involved in the decision process that measures the financial impact of varied manufacturing alternatives. If any operational change is made that affects a part's contribution, its routing, or the capacity of any constrained resource, the financial impact of that operational activity can be measured. Such changes are made to the data set, the "solve" command is given, and the optimal answer is instantaneously presented. Then the reader is prepared to enter the data for his or her particular plant or operation.

Maximum benefit will accrue to the reader who considers the whole text. However, due to the progressive nature of the text the reader will also derive benefits as the book is read and comprehended in stages. For example, the majority of the concepts are explained in chapters 1 through 4. Therefore, the reader should take a breather after Chapter 4 to ensure solid understanding before progressing to the elementary applications and then the more rigorous applications.

How It All Began

The OpTek Corporation in this text is a real industrial entity. The selling prices, variable costs, and routings have been altered but the product descriptions, that is, valve bodies, axle housings, differential cases, wheel hubs, and brake calipers, were actual parts. This company was founded over 150 years ago and is a world leader in the manufacture of agriculture and construction equipment. The company did in fact produce castings for their own use in the construction equipment industry and, as mentioned in the book, the agriculture equipment and over-the-road transportation industries too. During the time period when the concepts for this book were developed, annual sales for this company exceeded $2 billion.

The Oklahoma plant for the Foundry Products Division of this company was new in 1973 and was specifically designed for the company's casting requirements. The author was the plant's first controller and was subsequently assigned as operations manager.

The Foundry Products Division, not unlike other foundries, considered that weight was the proper unit of measure. Foundry capacity was expressed as tons per time period, and castings priced by the pound. The concepts introduced in this book revealed that this foundry, and in fact most foundries, were using a misleading unit of measure. Weight was definitely not the correct unit of measure for the foundry operations. The consequence was that all break-even calculations were meaningless, and foundry management had no idea of what financial expectations should be. The concepts introduced in this book revealed that the major constraint in the plant was the molding operation. That revelation required an entire new way to view the foundry operation. The author worked 10 years in this plant, where he developed and refined the concepts referred to in this book as optimization techniques. These concepts revealed that there were numerous (i.e., hundreds) of parts being made in the foundry that didn't fit relative to profit maximization. This new way of thinking further revealed where the marketing efforts should be focused.

The original algorithm is referred to in this book as the OpTek Algorithm and was initially programmed by one of the plant's systems analysts with the aid of a basic college algebra text. Optimization techniques were a major contributor in bringing the plant's break-even level from 80 percent capacity to 45 percent capacity in about a two-year time period. the plant manager, Mike Gray, said this of the concepts:

> "These concepts clearly pointed out which products best fit our facility to maximize our profit objective. We now excel worldwide with several products and have discontinued many other products due to Walt's recommendations."

SECTION I

Manufacturing Activities are Ultimately Expressed in Financial Terms

CHAPTER 1

Operational Improvements Don't Necessarily Translate to Financial Success

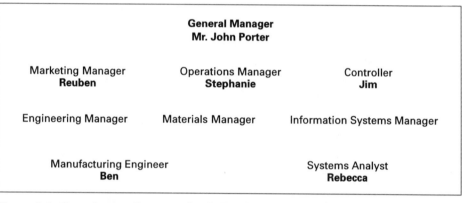

Figure 1.1 Organization Structure for OpTek Corporation. (The people named are active participants in the OpTek story.)

In the introductory chapter, the general manager of OpTek Corporation (John Porter) has recently come to a dreaded realization. His plant has been following concepts accepted as productive by manufacturers for years, but these have just been exposed as totally counterproductive relative to generating profit. Also, he has learned that operational improvements don't guarantee financial success.

He had just attended a workshop that introduced the *"Seven Deadly Sins of Manufacturing"* and returned with alternative contemporary financial measures. He was very enthusiastic about adopting these measures in his own plant. This chapter outlines the general manager's plan of action to implement the new concepts that he had just learned.

Chapter Contents

- The seven deadly sins of manufacturing
- Anticipating resistance to change
- Establishing the benchmark for measuring performance
- Clarification of the basic financial statements
- Capital productivity and ROI
- The ultimate objective—maximize ROI by adopting optimization techniques

OpTek Corporation's general manager, John Porter, was thinking about the seminar that he attended last week in Tulsa. The seminar introduced new financial metrics for manufacturers that were entirely new to him. He learned that the majority of manufacturers were involved in many counterproductive practices accepted for many years as being beneficial and, in fact, profit-enhancing. However, the seminar facilitator termed such practices as being downright counterproductive and *ineffective*. He defined ineffective as meaning that if such practices were being employed in a plant, that plant's ability to generate profit would be drastically curtailed. He said that the cost of the waste uncovered with traditional JIT and lean manufacturing was just the tip of the iceberg when compared with the magnitude of the waste associated with employing ineffective practices.

The Seven Deadly Sins of Manufacturing

With that explanation, the facilitator got very specific and said it was very counterproductive to:

1. Try to assess plant performance using an incorrect measure of capacity.
2. Use overhead absorption as a criterion for success in any way.
3. Focus on gross profit margins even if activity-based costing was used to establish product standard costs.
4. Focus on facility utilization.
5. Focus on cost minimization.
6. Focus on revenue maximization.
7. Develop a make-or-buy decision by comparing a part's total standard cost to make with the vendor's proposed price to supply it.

Then the facilitator said something that the general manager would never forget: **"If a plant focuses its attention on improving execution-based activities without addressing the basic sins of manufacturing, then that plant will be learning how to do the wrong things better."**

As OpTek's general manager, Mr. Porter, reviewed the list of the seven sins of manufacturing, he realized that his plant was guilty of participating in nearly all of them. The seminar made a believer out of him and he was totally convinced that his plant needed to adopt the optimization techniques introduced in Tulsa.

OpTek's senior staff consisted of Mr. Porter and three key players. They were Reuben, the marketing manager, Jim, the controller, and Stephanie, the operations manager. Each brought his or her own background and perspective to address OpTek's challenges. They were all well educated in their respective fields. Mr. Porter took pride in keeping himself and his staff current with contemporary management concepts. Stephanie held both CPIM and CIRM certifications and had attended several TOC workshops. Jim was a CPA and was a member of the Institute of Management Accountants. They had both been exposed to lean manufacturing concepts. Mr. Porter called a meeting of his staff to debrief them about his seminar last week relative to optimization technology that he had been introduced to:

> Our plant operates very well, but our overall financial performance is not where it needs to be. The work now flows smoothly through the shop, our inventories have been reduced by 60 percent and our on-time deliveries are at an all-time high. But there must be something basically wrong with the way we look at our operation. We're stuck at about a 5 percent ROI (return on investment). I used to think that if our operational performance improved then we would automatically see an improvement in our financials as well, but now I'm not so sure.

Anticipating Resistance to Change

"At the seminar that I attended last week, I was introduced to several new concepts that I feel will enhance our financial performance. Maybe we've been spending so much effort focusing on tactical execution that we're missing the big picture of what it really takes to increase our profit level."

At this point, Mr. Porter knew exactly where he intended to go. His challenge was to introduce his staff to the new level of performance measures, keeping in mind the magnitude of the required change in their thinking. His strategy would be to take on a facilitator role in the change process and thereby guide his staff in the transition from the traditional to the contemporary. He would achieve this objective by allowing them to expose the fallacies of current thinking as if they were plotting their own course. In this way, they would feel that they had actually discovered the new as they exposed the limitations of the old and would, therefore, take ownership in the change.

Establishing the Benchmark for Measuring Performance

"So we're going to begin the process of evaluating some of the basic premises on which we measure our performance. We need to begin, however, by defining a solid benchmark by which to measure our progress along the way. This benchmark will subsequently measure our ongoing performance as we begin to employ optimization techniques.

"Several years ago I attended a seminar designed for nonfinancial manufacturing professionals. I hadn't realized how relevant the concepts were until recently, as we strive to improve our financial performance while not really knowing quite how to go about it or how to measure the results of our efforts.

"Jim, consider that you have $5,000 invested in a money market account on the first day of 2003. When the first day of 2004 rolls around would you be happy to have the same $5,000 in that account? Of course not. You expect your money to grow for no other reason than the passage of time. The dimension of time is the benchmark by which we measure the growth of our money. Interest, simply defined, is the profit generated by letting someone else use our money and the calculation of interest expense is a function of time. Every personal loan whether for a house, car, or a small business, expresses the interest as APR (annual percentage rate). The same is true for those who have invested in our business. Consider that our plant has $400,000 in assets as of January 1, 2003 distributed as follows:

Table 1.1 OpTek's Beginning Balance Sheet January 1, 2003.

OpTek Corporation

Balance Sheet—January 1, 2003

Assets		Liabilities and Shareholders Equity	
Cash	$ 10		
Accounts receivable	25	Liabilities	100
Inventory	50		
Equipment	200	Shareholders equity (retained earnings)	300
Buildings	115		
Total assets	**$400**	**Total liabilities and shareholders equity**	**$400**

"Now let's say that our assets grow 5 percent, or $20 during the calendar year 2003 as follows:"

Table 1.2 The Relationship Between Profits Generated and Asset Growth

Beginning assets January 1, 2003	**+ $400**
Plus sales during 2003	+ $250
Minus costs during 2003	− $230
Profit generated during 2003	+ $ 20
Ending assets January 1, 2004	**= $420**

"Now, Jim, I fully realize that we can increase our assets in numerous other ways such as borrowing money or allowing our accounts payable to grow, but at this point our concern will be focused on *asset growth via profit generation*. Knowing both our beginning balance sheet for January 1, 2003 and our projected performance/activity during the year 2003, we can draft our projected balance sheet as of January 1, 2004."

Table 1.3 OpTek's Beginning Balance Sheet January 1, 2004.

OpTek Corporation

Balance Sheet—January 1, 2004

Assets		Liabilities and Shareholders Equity	
Cash	$ 30		
Accounts receivable	25	Liabilities	100
Inventory	50		
Equipment	200	Shareholders equity (retained earnings)	320
Buildings	115		
Total assets	**$420**	**Total liabilities and shareholders equity**	**$420**

"Our corporate performance relative to the time span is reflected in Figure 1.2."

Figure 1.2 OpTek's 2003 Performance Relative to the Time Span

Clarification of the Basic Financial Statements

"Figure 1.2 is both very basic but yet very profound. The figure is explained by the fact that it required one year to generate a profit of $20, or increase our asset base by 5 percent. The beginning point of $400 is known and the time period of one year is the *fixed benchmark*. The *variable* and subsequent challenge is how much *growth* of our assets (profit) can we generate with a given level of assets in the fixed time period benchmark of that year. This premise is at the very foundation of optimization technology.

"Our balance sheets, which list the level of our asset opportunity, are static as of specific dates. The increase in assets, or profit, is a dynamic function representing the growth of the assets over a time period (usually a year) and represents the activity between two balance sheets. The income statement reflects the change in assets or the profit of $20 in our case."

Capital Productivity and ROI

"Now we can readily calculate our projected capital productivity as well as our expected ROI":

$$\text{Productivity} = \frac{\text{Output}}{\text{Input}}$$

$$\text{Capital Productivity} = \frac{\text{Ending assets}}{\text{Beginning assets}} = \frac{\text{Output}}{\text{Input}} = \frac{\$420}{\$400} = 1.05$$

$$\text{ROI} = \frac{\text{Change in assets}}{\text{Beginning assets}} = \frac{\text{Profit}}{\text{Beginning assets}} = \frac{\$20}{\$400} = .05 = 5\%$$

"The similarity of capital productivity and ROI is readily evident."

The Ultimate Objective—Maximize ROI by Adopting Optimization Techniques

"As we measure our progress on the road to profit improvement, we'll measure the percent growth of our assets attributable to operating profit as an annual rate. Our asset opportunity will increase each year by the amount of profit generated during the year plus any additional capital equipment. *Our challenge will be to maximize our asset growth via profit generation at an annualized rate.* We will accomplish this by exposing and eliminating the counterproductive and ineffective performance measures that we presently use and replace them with relevant performance measures."

Summary—Key Points

OpTek's general manager realized that they had been traveling down a dead-end street. He discovered that any plant attempting to implement these new concepts should remember the following:

- All of the operational profit-maximizing improvements that can be implemented are useless as long as the plant is still participating in any of the "seven deadly sins of manufacturing."
- Resistance to change throughout a plant should be anticipated by the plant manager, and encouragement should be given to each department to work together to ensure success.
- Reaffirm that the "time dimension" should be the basic performance benchmark. Profit should be measured as a percent against asset opportunity over a given period of time, that is, per year.
- Clarify the plant's basic financial statements.
- Analyze the capital productivity and ROI for the plant.

The ultimate objectives are the following:

- To improve profit levels by weaning off the use of counterproductive practices and performance measures.
- To learn how to manage a plant and maximize ROI by following optimization techniques.

SECTION II

Exposing the Existing Counter-Productive Performance Measures

CHAPTER 2

The Standard Cost System: Manufacturing's Millstone

Mr. Porter began by assigning Jim, the controller, to evaluate their existing standard cost system. Jim would evaluate their present method of allocating overhead with a *single plantwide rate*, then assess the use of *departmental overhead rates* and, lastly, develop overhead rates using an *activity-based costing* system.

He would discover that each individual set of overhead rates required new product standard costs. He would also learn that such activities resulted in chasing variances.

This chapter will outline the emerging results of Jim's examination of the standard cost system to see if it actually relates to the process of improving manufacturing profitability.

Chapter Contents

- Identifying counterproductive things
- Appropriate measure of capacity
- Single plantwide rates → individual departmental overhead rates
- New product costs must follow overhead rate changes
- Incorporating new product costs
- New costs affect the desirability of each product
- Departmental overhead rates → activity-based costing
- Shifting fixed overhead allocations to different products has no value
- Adopting variable costing income statements is an effective thing to do

---

Identifying Counterproductive Things

"Let's begin with a review of our standard cost system. Jim, we've been arguing about the way we allocate and account for overhead for years now. Take a couple of weeks and evaluate our system. The proponents of optimization technology believe very strongly that overhead shouldn't even be allocated to products. See if you arrive at the same conclusion after your evaluation."

As Jim undertook his assignment he began by investigating different ways to more accurately apply the plant's fixed overhead to its product lines. Its monthly fixed overhead cost was $5,000 per Table 2.1.

Table 2.1 OpTek's Monthly Fixed Overhead Schedule

HVAC equipment lease	$ 400
Product engineering	1,000
Quality activities	1,500
Material handling	1,500
Setup	600
Total monthly fixed overhead	**$5,000**

OpTek made and sold five different products to five different markets. These product statistics are reflected in Table 2.2.

Table 2.2 Statistics for OpTek's Five Products

	Valve Body	Axle Housing	Differential Case	Wheel Hub	Brake Caliper
Selling price	$40.00	$42.50	$30.00	$35.00	$40.00
Variable cost*	25.00	20.00	20.00	17.50	21.00
Allocated fixed cost**	10.00	12.50	5.00	6.50	17.50
Gross profit	$ 5.00	$10.00	$ 5.00	$11.00	$ 1.50
Processing time	2.00 hrs	2.50 hrs	1.00 hrs	1.30 hrs	3.50 hrs

* Material, direct labor, and energy directly traceable to each product.

** OpTek's plant has five work centers with a monthly capacity of 200 hours each, resulting in a combined plant capacity of 1,000 processing hours. Therefore, the overhead rate was as follows:

$$\frac{\$5,000 \text{ total fixed overhead}}{1,000 \text{ total processing hours}} = \$5.00 \text{ per processing hour}$$

Example: The valve body requires 2 processing hours × $5.00 = $10.00 allocated fixed overhead.

Appropriate Measure of Capacity

OpTek had a machine-paced molding operation in its manufacturing process that limited its output to 400 total molds per month regardless of which product was in the mold. *Molding was the predominant production constraint and, therefore, the appropriate measure of capacity.* OpTek's existing strategy was to satisfy all five of its market segments; therefore, they made and sold 80 of each part per month, that is, 400 ÷ 5 = 80 each. Its monthly income statement is presented in Table 2.3.

Table 2.3 Typical Monthly Income Statement with 80 of Each Part

OpTek Corporation
Monthly Income Statement

Product	Qty.	Revenue	Variable Cost	Allocated Overhead	Gross Profit
Valve bodies	80	$ 3,200	$2,000	$ 800	$ 400
Axle housings	80	3,400	1,600	1,000	800
Differential cases	80	2,400	1,600	400	400
Wheel hubs	80	2,800	1,400	520	880
Brake calipers	80	3,200	1,680	1,400	120
Totals	400	$15,000	$8,280	$4,120	$2,600
			Less unabsorbed overhead ($5,000 – $4,120)		880
			Net operating profit		**$1,720**

Legend: Revenue = Quantity (80) × Selling price each from Table 2.2
Variable cost = Quantity (80) × Variable cost each from Table 2.2
Allocated overhead = Quantity (80) × Allocated overhead each from Table 2.2
Gross profit = Revenue – Variable cost – allocated overhead
Gross profit = Sales (revenue) – Total standard cost of sales

Jim knew that OpTek's production was sold in the month in which it was made and that allocated overhead also appeared in cost of sales in the same month. He also knew that the $4,120 allocated overhead did not include the total overhead actually incurred, that is, $5,000. Therefore, he knew that he had to subtract the unapplied amount of $880 from the gross profit amount in order to arrive at the *net operating profit*. The $5,000 monthly overhead is a fixed amount. If it is not all allocated, or absorbed, into inventory and subsequently into cost of sales, it must be recognized and expensed in the time period in which it occurred as a variance.

Single Plantwide Rates → Individual Departmental Overhead Rates

Jim wasn't comfortable with the overhead variance of $880. His reasoning was that inasmuch as the actual overhead expense was $5,000 per month and OpTek had settled into the product mix of 80 of each part, there should not be unabsorbed overhead, or variance. The total $5,000 should become part of the standard cost of sales instead of being classified as a variance. His remedy was to develop departmental overhead rates. He reasoned that a further benefit of departmental rates was that *Departmental overhead rates would certainly be more accurate than a single plant-wide overhead rate.* The first thing that Jim did was to examine the product routings through each department, as reflected in Table 2.4.

Table 2.4 Routing Matrix for OpTek Corporation

| | PRODUCT | | | | | |
Department	Valve Body	Axle Housing	Differential Case	Wheel Hub	Brake Caliper	Time Available
Core	.4	.8	.1	.3	.9	200 hrs.
Assembly	.7	.2	.1	.2	.7	200 hrs.
Molding	.5	.5	.5	.5	.5	200 hrs.
Cleaning	.1	.7	.2	.1	.6	200 hrs.
Grinding	.3	.3	.1	.2	.8	200 hrs.
Totals	2.0 hrs.	2.5 hrs.	1.0 hrs.	1.3 hrs.	3.5 hrs.	1,000 hrs.

The next step was to develop a resource utilization matrix based on the product mix of 80 of each part as shown in Table 2.5.

Table 2.5 Resource Utilization Matrix—Actual Department Loading Required to Support Making 80 of Each Part

Department	Valve Body		Axle Housing		Differential Case		Wheel Hub		Brake Caliper		
Core	80 [(.4)	+	(.8)	+	(.1)	+	(.3)	+	(.9)]	=	200
Assembly	80 [(.7)	+	(.2)	+	(.1)	+	(.2)	+	(.7)]	=	152
Molding	80 [(.5)	+	(.5)	+	(.5)	+	(.5)	+	(.5)]	=	200
Cleaning	80 [(.1)	+	(.7)	+	(.2)	+	(.1)	+	(.6)]	=	136
Grinding	80 [(.3)	+	(.3)	+	(.1)	+	(.2)	+	(.8)]	=	136
	80 [(2.0)	+	(2.5)	+	(1.0)	+	(1.3)	+	(3.5)]	=	824

Table 2.5 reveals that 824 processing hours were required to make 80 of each part. (This table is simply Table 2.4 multiplied by 80 of each part.) Comparing the 824 required hours with the 1,000 total available hours shows 176 hours not required, or idle capacity and 176 × $5.00 fixed overhead rate = $880 unabsorbed overhead, which agrees with Table 2.3.

With the information in Table 2.5 Jim was able to develop departmental overhead rates as follows in Table 2.6. He knew also that each department did in fact incur $1,000 of fixed overhead per month.

Table 2.6 Calculation of Departmental Overhead Rates Considering the Time Required to Produce 80 of Each Part and $1,000 Fixed Cost for Each Department

Core	= $1,000 ÷ 200 hours = $5.00 per hour
Assembly	= $1,000 ÷ 152 hours = $6.58 per hour
Molding	= $1,000 ÷ 200 hours = $5.00 per hour
Cleaning	= $1,000 ÷ 136 hours = $7.35 per hour
Grinding	= $1,000 ÷ 136 hours = $7.35 per hour

New Product Costs Must Follow Overhead Rate Changes

With the new departmental overhead rates Jim was now ready to develop new product standard costs. He begins with the valve body, as illustrated below in Table 2.7.

Table 2.7 Revised Standard Cost for the Valve Body Based on New Departmental Overhead Rates

Selling price		$40.00
Variable cost	25.00	
Fixed overhead		
Core .4($5.00) = $2.00		
Assembly .7($6.58) = 4.61		
Molding .5($5.00) = 2.50		
Cleaning .1($7.35) = 0.74		
Grinding .3($7.35) = 2.21		
	$12.06	
Total standard cost		$37.06
Gross profit		**$ 2.94**
The fixed overhead cost is calculated by multiplying the departmental times required by the valve body's routing, shown in Table 2.4, by the newly developed departmental overhead rates, shown in Table 2.6.		

Using this same methodology Jim proceeded to re-cost the other products being made and sold by OpTek.

Table 2.8 New Product Standard Costs Based on Departmental Overhead Rates

	Valve Body	Axle Housing	Differential Case	Wheel Hub	Brake Caliper
Selling price	$40.00	$42.50	$30.00	$35.00	$40.00
Variable cost	25.00	20.00	20.00	17.50	21.00
Fixed overhead					
Core	2.00	4.00	.50	1.50	4.50
Assembly	4.61	1.32	.66	1.32	4.61
Molding	2.50	2.50	2.50	2.50	2.50
Cleaning	.74	5.14	1.47	.74	4.41
Grinding	2.21	2.21	.74	1.47	5.58
Total fixed cost	12.06	15.17	5.87	7.53	21.90
Gross profit	$2.94	$7.33	$4.13	$9.97	($2.90)

Incorporating New Product Costs

Now Jim was ready to draft the pro forma monthly income statement reflecting the new product standard costs that incorporated departmental overhead rates applied to the product mix of 80 of each part (see Table 2.9 on page 19).

Jim quickly noted several things:

1. *Unabsorbed overhead*, or idle capacity variance, *was eliminated* using the departmental overhead rates and the existing product mix consisting of 80 of each part.
2. The result was in fact *more accurate product standard costs with the existing product mix.*
3. However, the net effect was that there was absolutely *no effect on profitability* when comparing the use of departmental overhead rates to using one general plantwide overhead rate. This would be expected as long as the product mix remained the same.

Table 2.9 Monthly Income Statement Based on Departmental Overhead Rates

OpTek Corporation

Monthly Income Statement

Product	Qty.	Revenue	Variable Cost	Allocated Fixed	Gross Profit
Valve bodies	80	$ 3,200	$2,000	$ 964	$ 236
Axle housings	80	3,400	1,600	1,213	587
Differential cases	80	2,400	1,600	469	331
Wheel hubs	80	2,800	1,400	602	798
Brake calipers	80	3,200	1,680	1,752	(232)
Totals	400	$15,000	$8,280	$5,000	$1,720
			Less unabsorbed overhead		0
			Net operating profit		$1,720

New Costs Affect the Desirability of Each Product

However, Jim did notice that the new product standard costs illustrated in Table 2.8 revealed that the brake caliper appeared to be a money loser, that is, each brake caliper sold indicated a loss of $2.90. He was a little surprised at his analysis and was quick to report his findings to Mr. Porter. Jim stated:

1. "We're losing $2.90 on every brake caliper that we sell."
2. "We make a profit of $9.97 on each wheel hub that we sell."
3. "I suggest that we stop making brake calipers and make more wheel hubs in their place."
4. "I'm confident of my analysis because I developed new standard costs based on individual departmental overhead rates."

Mr. Porter was very interested and instructed Jim to draft a pro forma income statement based on the following product mix:

Valve body	80 each
Axle housing	80 each
Differential case	80 each
Wheel hub	160 each
Brake calipers	0
Total parts	400 each

Jim was really enthused as he was trying to visualize the outcome before he put a pencil to the scenario. He reasoned that profits would increase by at least $1,000 per month:

Eliminate loss on 80 brake calipers × $2.90	= $	232
Increased profit with 80 additional wheel hubs × $9.97	= $	797
Estimated profit increase		**$1,029**

He drafted a revised pro forma income statement based on the new proposed product mix.

Table 2.10 Pro Forma Income Statement Using Departmental Overhead Rates, Eliminating Brake Calipers, and Replacing Them with Wheel Hubs

OpTek Corporation

Monthly Income Statement

Product	Qty.	Revenue	Variable Cost	Allocated Fixed Cost	Gross Profit
Valve bodies	80	$ 3,200	$2,000	$ 964	$ 236
Axle housings	80	3,400	1,600	1,213	587
Differential cases	80	2,400	1,600	469	331
Wheel hubs	160	5,600	2,800	1,204	1,596
Brake calipers	0	0	0	0	0
Totals	400	$14,600	$8,000	$3,850	$2,750
			Less unabsorbed overhead ($5,000 – $3,850)		– 1,150
			Net operating profit		$1,600

Jim was more than a little confused with the results. He had a hard time coming to grips with the fact that profits would decrease after developing more accurate product standard costs. He thought: *How in the world could we make less profit if we quit making 80 of a part that lost $2.90 each and replaced it with 80 of a part that had a gross profit of $9.97 each?* He reluctantly picked up the telephone and relayed his findings to Mr. Porter who thought to himself: There must be something basically wrong with the way we look at our business.

Departmental Overhead Rates → Activity Based Costing

Jim wasn't ready to discard the overhead question yet. He went back to square one with the product mix of 80 of each part. He decided to set up an activity-based costing (ABC) system. After months of careful analysis he came up with ABC rates for each product based on 80 of each part, or 400 total parts. The new ABC rates are listed in Table 2.11.

Table 2.11 Product Unit Fixed Cost Determined by ABC

Product	Facility-Level Cost	Product-Line-Level Cost	Batch-Level Cost	Total Unit Fixed Cost Per ABC[1]
Valve body	$1.00	$7.50	$1.75	$10.25
Axle housing	1.00	6.875	8.75	16.625
Differential case	1.00	1.875	7.00	9.875
Wheel hub	1.00	7.81	4.375	13.185
Brake caliper	1.00	7.19	4.375	12.565

With this new information, Jim prepared a monthly income statement:

Table 2.12 Income Statement Using ABC Rates and 80 of Each Product

OpTek Corporation
Monthly Income Statement

Product	Qty.	Revenue	Variable Cost	Allocated Fixed	Gross Profit
Valve bodies	80	$ 3,200	$2,000	$ 820	$ 380
Axle housings	80	3,400	1,600	1,330	470
Differential cases	80	2,400	1,600	790	10
Wheel hubs	80	2,800	1,400	1,055	345
Brake calipers	80	3,200	1,680	1,005	515
Totals	400	$15,000	$8,280	$5,000	1,720
			Less unabsorbed overhead		0
			Net operating profit		$1,720

---

1 The detailed construction of the ABC rates is found in Appendix A at the end of this book.

Several things became very clear to Jim when he compared the different income statements using varied overhead rates:

1. All of the $5,000 monthly fixed overhead would be absorbed with both departmental rates and ABC rates.
2. Allocated overhead and gross profit per product varied greatly when the overhead rates varied.
3. The total plant operating profit, however, did not change as the overhead rates changed with the same product mix of 80 of each part.

Shifting Fixed Overhead Allocations to Different Products Has No Value

Jim determined that there was no financial benefit resulting from allocating or assigning fixed period overhead costs to products. He also realized that disastrous decisions could be made when products are added or deleted from the product mix based on the fixed overhead allocated to them regardless of the sophistication of the method used in the allocation/assignment process. He considered the wheel hub as an example. The total standard cost for this part varied greatly, depending on the method of overhead allocation chosen. If prices were established on percent markup, then the problem is compounded. Consider that OpTek wanted to establish the price for the wheel hub based on 20 percent markup over total product standard cost.

Product: **Wheel Hub**

Overhead Allocation Method	Variable Cost	Allocated Fixed Cost	Total Cost	20% Markup	Suggested Selling Price
One plantwide rate	$17.50	$ 6.50	$24.00	$4.80	$28.80
Departmental rates.	17.50	7.53	25.03	5.01	30.04
ABC determined rates	17.50	13.19	30.69	6.14	36.83

The increase in the price of this item has not added one iota of value either in reality or perception in the eyes of the customer. The market and the customer's perception of value will determine what that customer is willing to pay. There appeared to be no value in allocating the $5,000 monthly fixed overhead to products. Such a practice implies that fixed costs are unit driven. Jim decided that *the concept of fixed cost per unit was not valid and certainly not conducive to increasing total plant profits.*

Adopting Variable Costing Income Statements Is an Effective Thing to Do

At this point, Jim made a major decision. OpTek would no longer allocate fixed overhead to products. The concept of overhead absorption would be thrown out the window and the monthly fixed overhead cost of $5,000 would be handled as a single amount on their income statements. OpTek would adopt the variable costing income statement format for presenting operating profits, as reflected in Table 2.13.

Table 2.13 OpTek's Monthly Income Statement in the Variable Costing Format with 80 of Each Product

OpTek Corporation
Variable Costing Income Statement

Product	Qty.	Revenue	Variable Cost	Contribution
Valve bodies	80	$3,200	$2,000	$1,200
Axle housings	80	3,400	1,600	1,800
Differential cases	80	2,400	1,600	800
Wheel hubs	80	2,800	1,400	1,400
Brake calipers	80	3,200	1,680	1,520
Totals	400	$15,000	$8,280	$6,720
Less monthly fixed cost				5,000
Net operating profit				$1,720

Jim had completed the first phase of investigating the overhead question, but he wasn't ready to report back to Mr. Porter yet. He asked himself how something that had been used for so many years could be so counterproductive.

Summary—Key Points

As plant overhead rates are developed using more sophisticated methods, the results are basically the same. The key points to remember are the following:

- Begin by identifying the "wrong" counterproductive and ineffective practices within the plant.
- Determine the appropriate measure of plant capacity.
- Total overhead absorption has absolutely no effect on profitability.
- Different overhead rates necessitate new product standard costs—if a plant develops its pricing structure based on marking up product standard costs, its prices will vary according to the method of overhead allocation.
- Customers are not sensitive to a producer's need to cover overhead expenses. They are willing to pay only the market-determined price.
- Shifting fixed overhead allocations to different products has no value, so should not be followed.

Conclusions

- Overhead absorption has to go.
- The variable costing income statement format should be adopted.

CHAPTER 3

Maximizing Gross Profit: Introduction to Optimization Techniques

This chapter reveals that if a plant is able to improve its level of gross profit, there is no indication that net operating profit will also improve. It will be illustrated that there is no relationship between the two.

Jim wasn't ready yet to accept that more accurate product standard costs didn't contribute to increased profitability. After proving that overhead absorption had no affect on profitability, he reasoned that perhaps *focusing on gross profit was a better objective*. He further reasoned that individual part gross profit statistics would be more accurate as that part's individual standard cost became more accurate. So he set out to prove that by maximizing total plant gross profit based on the most accurate product standard costs, he would find the answer to net profit improvement.

Chapter Contents

- Introduction to optimization techniques
- Gross profit has no direct relationship to net operating profit
- The limited value of activity-based costing

At this point, a light came on in Jim's mind. He reasoned that the more accurate the product standard costs, the more accurate each product's respective gross profit calculation. Perhaps the advantage of more accurate product standard costs was not found in maximizing overhead absorption, but rather in maximizing gross profit. He thought: Maybe we've misplaced our focus on overhead absorption, which we've discovered has no affect on total plant profitability. However, he had no idea how to determine the product mix that would maximize total plant gross profit within the confines of their plant's work center capacities and product routings. He presented that challenge to one of OpTek's systems analysts.

Introduction to Optimization Techniques

Optimization technology is not new. However, its widespread use in manufacturing operations has not grown as fast as some other aspects of manufacturing improvements, that is, lean manufacturing. This book will illustrate, however, that the benefits of lean manufacturing cannot be fully realized without the incorporation of optimization technology. As mentioned in the preface to this book, the application of lean activities combined with any of the "seven deadly sins of manufacturing" will produce diluted results at best.

Optimization techniques have been employed in the Theory of Constraints on a tactical level. However, its application in this book begins with the formulation of a plant's strategy. It is one thing to formulate a feasible strategy; it is quite another to formulate the optimum strategy. In other words, the strategy, that will result in the maximum possible profit.

OpTek's analyst, Rebecca, met with Jim to explain the magnitude of his request and to tell him all that would be needed to develop an optimization model that would indicate what OpTek's product mix must be to provide the maximum possible total plant gross profit. Rebecca explained that many variables needed to be considered simultaneously, such as each product's gross profit, each product's routing, and each department's capacity. After about a month, she did, however, develop such a model and called it the OpTek Algorithm, (see Appendix B, pp. 193–204). Jim was about to get his first exposure to optimization technology. Such reasoning transcends the pursuit of local activities so typical of managing with a standard cost system, and instead *focuses on the performance of the total plant.*

Rebecca explained to Jim that the algorithm begins with an objective. In the present case, the objective would be to maximize total plant gross profit. Inasmuch as the objective is to maximize total plant gross profit, Jim must consider each product's respective gross profit. He remembered the calculation of each product's gross profit on Table 2.2 (p. 14).

Product	Gross Profit
Valve body	$ 5.00
Axle housing	10.00
Differential case	5.00
Wheel hub	11.00
Brake caliper	1.50

Therefore, the objective is:

**Maximize $5.00(valve body) + $10.00(axle housing) + $5.00(differential case) +
$11.00(wheel hub) + $1.50(brake caliper)**

(Subject to product routings and departmental capacities per Table 2.4. [p. 16]).

The OpTek Algorithm will determine the product mix, i.e., the number of each product that will produce the highest possible total plant gross profit. Jim activates the algorithm in his PC and the results are presented in Table 3.1.

Table 3.1 Output Format for the OpTek Algorithm with the Objective of Maximizing Total Plant Gross Profit

Product	Qty.	Department	Hrs. Required	Slack	Opportunity
Valve bodies	0	Core	120	80	0
Axle housings	0	Assembly	80	120	0
Differential cases	0	Molding	200	0	$22.00
Wheel hubs	400	Cleaning	40	160	0
Brake calipers	0	Grinding	80	120	0
Totals	400		520	480	
Maximum gross profit possible $4,400 (*See Appendix B*)					

Legend for Table 3.1:

Qty. = The number of each product required to achieve the objective

Hrs. Required = The number of hours required in each department to produce the products in the Qty. column.

Example: The routing of the wheel hub from Table 2.4:
Core = .3(400)Qty = 120
Assembly = .2(400)Qty = 80
Molding = .5(400)Qty = 200
Cleaning = .1(400)Qty = 40
Grinding = .2(400)Qty = 80

Slack: Core time available = 200 – 120 required = 80 slack
Assembly time available = 200 – 80 required = 120 slack
Molding time available = 200 – 200 required = 0 slack
Cleaning time available = 200 – 40 required = 160 slack
Grinding time available = 200 – 80 required = 120 slack

Opportunity: There will only be an entry in this column if there is 0 slack, such as in molding in the present example. This number represents the amount of additional gross profit, i.e., the present objective, that the plant could achieve if the molding capacity was increased by one more hour of available time. Remember that each mold requires .5 hours. Therefore, one additional hour would allow for two additional molds. Inasmuch as the gross profit for each wheel hub is $11.00, the additional opportunity with one more hour of molding capacity would be 2 × $11.00 = $22.00, as shown. Opportunity exists only when a constraint exists. There is no opportunity by adding time to departmental capacity if the department already has idle capacity.

Maximum Value of the Objective: Last, the maximum gross profit that OpTek's plant could generate with existing conditions is $4,400 per month, which is 400 wheel hubs × its individual gross profit of $11.00 each.

Jim was really excited about this new tool. He imagined doing all sorts of planning and budgeting with it. He decided, however, to play around with the algorithm before showing it to the other staff members.

Gross Profit Has No Direct Relationship to Net Operating Profit

Jim had learned previously that gross profit didn't equate with net operating profit if there was any unabsorbed overhead (idle capacity variance). So he took the product mix defined by gross profit maximization illustrated in Table 3.1 and expressed it in the variable costing income statement format introduced in Table 2.13 (p. 23) in order to calculate net operating profit.

Table 3.2 Monthly Operating Profit with 400 Wheel Hubs

OpTek Corporation
Variable Costing Income Statement

Product	Qty.	Revenue	Variable Cost	Contribution
Wheel hubs	400	$14,000	$7,000	$7,000
		Less monthly fixed cost		5,000
		Net operating profit		**$2,000**

Jim was very encouraged. The net operating profit when producing the product mix that maximized gross profit exceeded the $1,720 when producing an equal number of each part, OpTek's existing strategy. Then he remembered that their product standard costs were the most accurate after they developed overhead rates derived from the ABC system. This, he reasoned, would naturally result in the most accurate product gross profit calculations. So the next thing that Jim did was enter the gross profit calculations derived from the ABC system into the algorithm. Individual product gross profits derived from ABC are developed in Table 3.3:

Table 3.3 Individual Product Gross Profits Derived from ABC-Determined Rates

Product	Selling Price	Variable Cost	ABC Fixed Cost*	Gross Profit
Valve body	$40.00	$25.00	$10.25	$4.75
Axle housing	42.50	20.00	16.63	5.87
Differential case	30.00	20.00	9.88	.12
Wheel hub	35.00	17.50	13.19	4.31
Brake caliper	40.00	21.00	12.57	6.43

* from Table 2.11

Now maximum plant gross profit using ABC-determined rates can be determined:

Maximize **$4.75(valve body) + $5.87(axle housing) + $.12(differential case) + $4.31(wheel hub) +$6.43(brake caliper)**

(Subject to product routings and departmental capacities per Table 2.4.)

The results are reflected in Table 3.4.

Table 3.4 Maximum Plant Gross Profit Using ABC-Derived Overhead Rates

Objective: **Maximize Gross Profit**					
Product	Qty.	Department	Hrs. Required	Slack	Opportunity
Valve bodies	128	Core	200	0	$3.36
Axle housings	0	Assembly	200	0	.21
Differential cases	0	Molding	200	0	6.52
Wheel hubs	160	Cleaning	96	104	0
Brake calipers	112	Grinding	160	40	0
Totals	400		856	144	
Maximum Gross Profit Possible $2,018					

One of the first things that Jim noticed was that plant utilization had greatly improved even though total gross profit had decreased. Plant utilization was just 52 percent (520 ÷ 1,000) in Table 3.1, while it is 85.6 percent in Table 3.4. He realized, however, that he really couldn't interpret these results without presenting this product mix in the variable costing income statement format per Table 3.5.

Table 3.5 Net Operating Profit by Maximizing Gross Profit Using ABC Determined Overhead Rates

OpTek Corporation

Variable Costing Income Statement

Product	Qty.	Revenue	Variable Cost	Contribution
Valve bodies	128	$5,120	$3,200	$1,920
Wheel hubs	160	5,600	2,800	2,800
Brake calipers	112	4,480	2,352	2,128
Totals	400	$15,200	$8,352	$6,848
Less monthly fixed cost				5,000
Net operating profit				$1,848

Now Jim was really confused. He had discovered that the maximum gross profit generated with the product mix, which used the most accurate product standard costs developed with ABC, i.e., Table 3.4, was actually less than the gross profit possible when using product standard costs developed using one overall plantwide overhead rate per Table 3.1. It was also confirmed again that plant gross profit has little relationship to net operating profit.

	Plant Gross Profit	produced	Plant Net Profit
Tables 3.1 and 3.2	$4,400		$2,000
Tables 3.4 and 3.5	$2,018		$1,848

With tongue in cheek, he decided to make one additional analysis, i.e., the determination of how much of the plant overhead would actually be absorbed with this latest scenario. He thought that knowing this would perhaps shed some light on the matter, especially since plantwide utilization had improved. For this analysis he had to go back to Table 3.3 to find the overhead allocated per unit with ABC, and then multiply the overhead cost per unit times the quantity of products in Table 3.5.

Table 3.6 Overhead Absorbed with Product Mix That Maximizes Plant Gross Profit with ABC-Derived Overhead Rates

Product	Qty. in Mix (Table 3.5)	Overhead Allocated to Each (Table 3.3)	Total Overhead Absorbed
Valve bodies	128	$10.25	$1,312
Wheel hubs	160	13.19	2,110
Brake calipers	112	12.57	1,408
Totals	400		$4,830

This was amazing! The percent of overhead absorbed using ABC-derived overhead rates was 96.6 percent ($4,830 ÷ $5,000) and yet net operating profit decreased from $2,000 per Table 3.2 to $1,848 per Table 3.5. This latest finding definitely confirmed Jim's earlier decision to forever abandon the concept of overhead absorption. It only led to confusion with no accompanying financial benefit.

Gross profit maximization did not lead to net operating profit maximization! Even using the most accurate possible product standard costs developed with ABC methods, the pursuit of gross profit maximization proves to have no value. Overhead allocation to products appears to have little value unless used for inventory valuation to satisfy external reporting requirements at the end of a fiscal period.

One final note on overhead absorption: Jim learned that when overhead absorption is an overt objective, the driver that is activated to absorb overhead may be pursued to the detriment of the total plant. If, for example, direct labor is the driver to absorb overhead, more direct labor hours worked may lessen the overhead (idle capacity) variance. The pursuit to increase departmental utilization and decrease idle capacity variance may lead to dysfunctional behavior. The end result is an increase in WIP inventory at the expense of total plant financial improvement. He reasoned that: *Idle inventory is much **more** a sin than idle capacity.*

The Limited Value of Activity-Based Costing

Last, perhaps the most significant benefit of ABC is that it forces a plant to examine in detail the overhead expenses incurred in that plant, which should lead to subsequent monitoring and control. *While ABC may produce the most accurate product standard costs, there is no direct relationship between standard cost accuracy and operating profit enhancement.*

The focus on gross profit maximization as well as leaning on ABC for improving net operating profit proved to be counterproductive.

Summary—Key Points

We have learned that overhead absorption has no relevance to improving net operating profit, this chapter has also:

- Introduced us to optimization techniques, i.e., a device to determine a plant's product mix, which produces maximum total gross profit (or any other objective).
- Illustrated there is no relationship between a plant's gross profit and its net operating profit.

But even with optimization techniques, we have discovered that:

- There is no direct relationship between product standard cost accuracy and plant profitability.
- Product standard costs developed with activity-based methodology have no direct bearing on plant profitability.

This would be an appropriate time to read Appendix B, "Using Excel Solver to Execute the OpTek Algorithm" (pp. 193–204).

Maximizing Return on Investment (R.O.I) is the Ultimate Objective: How to Get There is the Great Challenge

CHAPTER 4

Which Operational Objective Will Produce the Most Profit?

Up to this point we have learned that the standard cost system (including activity-based costing) is absolutely no help in pointing us in the direction of increased profitability. In the continuing story of OpTek, Mr. Porter, the general manager, will solicit his staff to suggest other ideas to improve profitability. Each staff member will suggest objectives relative to their own perspectives. Reuben, the marketing manager, will suggest that profit improvement is a function of revenue maximization while Stephanie, the operations manager, will suggest an objective that maximizes plant utilization. Other objectives suggested will include cost minimization and throughput maximization. These objectives will be simulated using the new optimization device, the OpTek Algorithm.

Chapter Contents

- OpTek's existing financial performance statistics: productivity of capital/ROI and break-even level
- Different functional managers have different ideas on how to improve profits
- The relationship between revenue and profitability
- The relationship between cost and profitability
- The relationship between plant utilization and profitability
- The relationship between throughput and profitability
- Revenue/cost relationships and profitability
- Summarizing the results
- Measuring the improvement of OpTek's financial performance

Jim may have had the OpTek Algorithm at his disposal, but it sure hadn't helped him yet learn how to maximize net operating profits at the plant. He knew that the overall goal was to maximize net operating profits, but knowing the appropriate strategy to achieve that goal was not as obvious. His experience with overhead absorption and gross profit maximization eliminated both of them as viable objectives in the quest to increase net operating profit.

OpTek's Existing Financial Performance Statistics: Productivity of Capital/ROI and Break-Even Level

The OpTek plant had net assets totaling $400,000, and its present net profit was $1,720 per month, or $20,640 annually, by producing 80 of each part to satisfy all five of their markets. Table 2.13 (p. 23) also revealed that OpTek's contribution with this strategy was $6,720 per month. With this information, OpTek can determine its existing primary financial status:

$$\textbf{Capital Productivity: } \frac{\text{Ending assets}}{\text{Beginning assets}} = \frac{\text{Output}}{\text{Input}} = \frac{\$420,640^*}{\$400,000} = 1.0516$$

* $1,720 Monthly Profit $\times$ 12 = $20,640 annual profit + $400,000 Beginning Assets = $420,640 = Output, or ending assets

$$\textbf{ROI: } \frac{\text{Ending assets} - \text{Beginning assets}}{\text{Beginning assets}} = \frac{\text{Profit}}{\text{Beginning assets}} = \frac{\$20,640}{\$400,000} = 5.16\%$$

Break-Even Level:

$$\frac{\$6,720 \text{ contribution}}{400 \text{ total molds (primary constraint)}} = \$16.80 \text{ contribution per mold}$$

$$\frac{\$5,000 \text{ total monthly fixed cost}}{\$16.80 \text{ contribution per mold}} = 297 \text{ molds to break even}$$

$$\frac{297 \text{ molds to break even}}{400 \text{ total molds capacity}} = 74.25\% \text{ mold capacity to break even}$$

Mr. Porter knew that 5.16 percent ROI was not acceptable for their industry. He was convinced that they could improve it but he was not sure how to go about it. He was totally open to the idea that perhaps they were still involved in counterproductive practices that inhibited their ability to improve their net operating profit. He considered that perhaps their product mix strategy was wrong. He reconvened his senior staff, i.e., marketing manager, Reuben, operations manager,

Stephanie, and of course controller, Jim. As they were sitting around the conference table they begin to list the feasible strategies available to them.

Different Functional Managers Have Different Ideas on How to Improve Profits

Reuben began from the marketing perspective of suggesting that if they could increase revenue, they would certainly increase profit because they would establish prices based on marking up total product standard costs. He reasoned further that additional revenue would leverage the $5,000 monthly fixed cost, which would remain constant. Jim silently cringed as he remembered his previous bad experience with total product standard costs, which had included allocated overhead.

However, Jim did counter from his own perspective and suggested that profits are a result of cost minimization. There is really no question about it. The product mix that minimizes cost will automatically maximize profit.

Stephanie had not yet learned the same lesson that Jim had about overhead absorption. She persisted in believing that the product mix that generated the greatest amount of direct labor hours would result in profit maximization. Her thinking was that the more standard hours earned the more overhead that would be absorbed: The more overhead absorbed, the less will be the unabsorbed overhead, and, logically, the higher will be our profits.

Armed with the OpTek Algorithm, they began to evaluate their respective ideas to see which objective would in fact generate the highest level of net operating profit for their plant.

The Relationship Between Revenue and Profitability

Reuben was first with his proposal of increasing revenue. Therefore, the objective for the algorithm became revenue maximization. This objective required the examination of the selling price of each product.

Table 4.1 Individual Product's Selling Price

Product	Selling Price Each from Table 2.2 (p. 14)
Valve body	$40.00
Axle housing	42.50
Differential case	30.00
Wheel hub	35.00
Brake caliper	40.00

They activated the algorithm with the following objective:

Maximize $40.00(valve body) + $42.50(axle housing) + $30.00(differential case) + $35.00(wheel hub) + $40.00(brake caliper)

(Subject to the product routings and departmental capacities in Table 2.4 [p. 16].)

Table 4.2 Product Mix Required for Revenue Maximization

Objective: **Maximize Revenue**					
Product	**Qty.**	**Department**	**Hrs. Required**	**Slack**	**Opportunity**
Valve bodies	240	Core	200.00	0	$15.00
Axle housings	112	Assembly	200.00	0	7.00
Differential cases	0	Molding	200.00	0	58.20
Wheel hubs	48	Cleaning	107.20	92.80	0
Brake calipers	0	Grinding	115.20	84.80	0
Totals	**400**		**822.40**	**177.60**	
Maximum revenue possible $16,040					

The next step was to express the above product mix information in income statement format.

Table 4.3 Net Operating Profit for the Product Mix That Maximizes Revenue

OpTek Corporation
Variable Costing Income Statement

Product	**Qty.**	**Revenue**	**Variable Cost**	**Contribution**
Valve bodies	240	$9,600 (240 × $40.00)	$6,000 (240 × $25.00)	$3,600
Axle housings	112	4,760 (112 × $42.50)	2,240 (112 × 20.00)	2,520
Wheel hubs	48	1,680 (48 × $35.00)	840 (48 × 17.50)	840
Totals	**400**	**$16,040**	**$9,080**	**$6,960**
		Less facility fixed cost		5,000
		Net operating profit		$1,960

All of them studied the results very carefully because this was the first exposure that several of them had to optimization technology. They noted the following:

1. The resulting profit from maximizing revenue is indeed more than with their existing mix, where 80 of each part was produced. Profit increased from $1,720 per Table 2.13 to $1,960 in Table 4.3.
2. This product mix included only three of the five products that OpTek was presently making.
3. This product mix reveals that three departments would be constrained with this strategy per Table 4.2.

Department	Slack	Opportunity
Core	0	$15.00
Assembly	0	7.00
Molding	0	58.20

Reuben was pleased inasmuch as his proposal would produce more profit than if he used OpTek's existing strategy of producing an equal number of each part.

The Relationship Between Cost and Profitability

Now it was time to evaluate Jim's suggestion to minimize total cost. Inasmuch as their fixed cost was $5,000 per month, regardless of the product mix, the objective would be to minimize variable cost, which would automatically minimize total plant cost. The input required the variable cost of each of the products.

Table 4.4 Variable Cost of Each of the Products from Table 2.2

Product	Variable Cost Table 2.2
Valve body	$25.00
Axle housing	20.00
Differential case	20.00
Wheel hub	17.50
Brake caliper	21.00

The objective in this case is:

Minimize $25.00(valve body) + $20.00(axle housing) + $20.00(differential case) + $17.50(wheel hub) + $21.00(brake caliper)

(Subject to the product routings and departmental capacities in Table 2.4.)

The product mix that satisfies the cost minimization objective is found in Table 4.5

Table 4.5 Product Mix for Variable Cost Minimization

Objective: **Minimize Variable Cost**					
Product	Qty.	Department	Hrs. Required	Slack	Opportunity
Valve bodies	0	Core	120	80	0
Axle housings	0	Assembly	80	120	0
Differential cases	0	Molding	200	0	–$35.00
Wheel hubs	400	Cleaning	40	160	0
Brake calipers	0	Grinding	80	120	0
Totals	400		520	480	
Minimum variable cost possible $7,000					

They quickly expressed this product mix in income statement format:

Table 4.6 Net Operating Profit When Variable Cost Is Minimized

OpTek Corporation
Variable Costing Income Statement

Product	Qty.	Revenue	Variable Cost	Contribution
Wheel hubs	400	$14,000	$7,000	$7,000
		Less monthly fixed cost		5,000
		Net operating profit		$2,000

Once again, they noted several interesting things about this scenario:

1. The resulting profit with cost minimization is more than with either:
   (a) making an equal number of each part, i.e., $1,720 per Table 2.13.
   (b) maximization of revenue, i.e., $1,960 per Table 4.3.
2. The revenue for the cost minimizing mix, $14,000, is substantially less than with the revenue maximizing mix, i.e., $16,040.
3. While *profit increased*, total *plant utilization decreased* dramatically.

Utilization with revenue maximizing mix: $\dfrac{\text{Hrs. required}}{\text{Hrs. available}} = \dfrac{822.40}{1,000} = 82.24\%$

Utilization with cost minimizing mix: $\dfrac{\text{Hrs. required}}{\text{Hrs. available}} = \dfrac{520}{1,000} = 52.00\%$

At this point Jim was pleased because his suggestion resulted in more operating profit than with Reuben's suggestion to maximize revenue.

All of a sudden another light went on in Jim's mind. He remembered that the mix of 400 wheel hubs that minimized variable cost was the same mix that maximized gross profit. That can't be a coincidence, thought Jim. *If gross profit is the highest when costs are the lowest, the mix of 400 wheel hubs must be the most profitable mix for us.* So he couldn't help but blurt out: "We need to be a wheel hub producer!"

"We're not ready to make that decision," said Mr. Porter. "We haven't heard from Stephanie yet."

The Relationship Between Plant Utilization and Profitability

Remember, Stephanie thought that plant utilization was the answer. Now she was a little hesitant after seeing the results of cost minimization, where profit actually increased as utilization decreased. Anyway, she wasn't ready to back off from her argument without further proof. In order to maximize plant utilization Stephanie had to review the required processing time per product back in Table 2.2.

Table 4.7 Total Processing Time Required for Each Product from Table 2.2

Product	Total Processing Time Required
Valve body	2.0 hrs.
Axle housing	2.5 hrs.
Differential case	1.0 hrs.
Wheel hub	1.3 hrs.
Brake caliper	3.5 hrs.

The objective became:

Maximize 2.0 hrs(valve body) + 2.5 hrs(axle housing) + 1.0 hr(differential case) + 1.3 hrs(wheel hub) + 3.5 hrs(brake caliper)

(Subject to the product routings and departmental capacities in Table 2.4.)

The resulting product mix is reflected in Table 4.8.

Table 4.8 Product Mix Required to Maximize Plant Utilization

Objective: **Maximize Plant Utilization**					
Product	Qty.	Department	Hrs. Required	Slack	Opportunity
Valve bodies	107	Core	200.00	0	3.00
Axle housings	0	Assembly	200.00	0	.17
Differential cases	133	Molding	200.00	0	1.37
Wheel hubs	0	Cleaning	133.33	66.67	0
Brake calipers	160	Grinding	173.33	26.67	0
Totals	400		906.66	93.34	
Maximum plant utilization possible 90.67%					

The variable costing income statement representing the product mix for maximum plant utilization follows in Table 4.9.

Table 4.9 Net Operating Profit When Plant Utilization Is Maximized

OpTek Corporation

Variable Costing Income Statement

Product	Qty.	Revenue	Variable Cost	Contribution
Valve bodies	107	$4,280	$2,675	$1,605
Differential cases	133	3,990	2,660	1,330
Brake calipers	160	6,400	3,360	3,040
Totals	400	$14,670	$8,695	$5,975
		Less facility fixed cost		5,000
		Net operating profit		$ 975

Needless to say, they were all stunned. The obvious question then arose: what was the relationship between plant utilization and profitability? Apparently, none.

They noted several other interesting facts.

1. The facility utilization was indeed higher than with any other strategy:

$$\text{Plant utilization} = \frac{\text{Total hours required}}{\text{Total available hours}} = \frac{906.66}{1,000} = 90.67\%$$

2. The resulting product mix was substantially different than with any of the other proposed mixes.
3. The resulting profit was a disaster compared with the previous mixes.

At this point, they were about to accept the $2,000 net operating profit provided with the strategy of cost minimization.

The Relationship Between Throughput and Profitability

Then Mr. Porter commented that he had read a book recently that introduced a measure of performance called *throughput*. He read the definition directly from the book so as not to misquote the authors:

> **Throughput = the quantity of money generated by the firm through sales over a specified period of time.**
>
> **Throughput is equal to sales revenue minus the material cost of goods sold.**

Mr. Porter then turned to Jim and asked if their product standard cost information listed material as a separate item. Jim indicated that this information was readily available, and then proceeded to prepare a table reflecting each product's selling price, the standard cost of each product's material content, and the resulting throughput value of each product per Table 4.10.

Table 4.10 The Calculation of Each Product's Throughput Value

Product	Selling Price	Standard Cost of Material	Throughput Value
Valve body	$40.00	$ 2.50	$37.50
Axle housing	42.50	4.00	38.50
Differential case	30.00	6.00	24.00
Wheel hub	35.00	7.00	28.00
Brake caliper	40.00	10.50	29.50

Thinking that they had found the answer to profit maximization, they quickly activated the OpTek Algorithm using throughput maximization as the objective:

Maximize $37.50(valve body) + $38.50(axle housing) + $24.00(differential case) + $28.00(wheel hub) + $29.50(brake caliper)

(Subject to the product routings and departmental capacities in Table 2.4.)

The product mix that maximized throughput is found below in Table 4.11.

Table 4.11 Product Mix That Maximizes Throughput

Objective: **Maximize Throughput**					
Product	Qty.	Department	Hrs. Required	Slack	Opportunity
Valve bodies	246	Core	200.00	0	$18.84
Axle housings	123	Assembly	200.00	0	13.07
Differential cases	31	Molding	200.00	0	41.61
Wheel hubs	0	Cleaning	116.93	83.07	0
Brake calipers	0	Grinding	113.85	86.15	0
Totals	400		830.78	169.22	
Maximum throughput possible $14,705					

Expressing this product mix in the variable costing income statement format produces Table 4.12.

Table 4.12 Net Operating Profit When Maximizing Throughput

OpTek Corporation

Variable Costing Income Statement

Product	Qty.	Revenue	Variable Cost	Contribution
Valve bodies	246	$9,840	$6,150	$3,690
Axle housings	123	5,228	2,460	2,768
Differential cases	31	930	620	310
Totals	400	$15,998	$9,230	$6,768
Less monthly fixed cost				5,000
Net operating profit				$1,768

Their disappointment was visible as they analyzed the results. *Throughput maximization did not produce the highest net operating profit, but this product mix did produce the highest variable cost* of any of the previous scenarios. They realized that the $1,768 net operating profit provided with this latest scenario was not much different than the $1,720 net operating profit provided with their existing strategy of producing 80 of each part.

Revenue/Cost Relationships and Profitability

Then Mr. Porter began to note a pattern: "Our fixed cost will be the same for any product mix; therefore, profitability appears to be a function of revenue and variable costs. Maximum revenue didn't produce the highest profit, nor did minimum cost. I wonder what would happen if we determined the product mix that produced the greatest distance between revenue and variable cost, i.e., maximum contribution." The others shrugged and thought they had nothing to lose by trying this strategy.

The first thing Jim had to do was tabulate each part's contribution:

Table 4.13 Determination of Each Part's Individual Contribution

Product	SellingPrice/Each	Variable Cost/Each	Contribution/ Each
Valve body	$40.00	$25.00	$15.00
Axle housing	42.50	20.00	22.50
Differential case	30.00	20.00	10.00
Wheel hub	35.00	17.50	17.50
Brake caliper	40.00	21.00	19.00

The objective for contribution maximization became:

Maximize $15.00(valve body) + $22.50(axle housing) + $10.00(differential case) + $17.50(wheel hub) + $19.00(brake caliper)

(Subject to the product routings and departmental capacities in Table 2.4.)

Table 4.14 Product Mix That Maximizes Contribution

Objective: **Maximize Contribution**					
Product	Qty.	Department	Hrs. Required	Slack	Opportunity
Valve bodies	0	Core	200	0	$10.00
Axle housings	160	Assembly	80	120	0
Differential cases	0	Molding	200	0	29.00
Wheel hubs	240	Cleaning	136	64	0
Brake calipers	0	Grinding	96	104	0
Totals	400		712	288	
Maximum contribution possible $7,800					

This product mix was then expressed in the variable costing income statement format per Table 4.15.

Table 4.15 Net Operating Profit When Maximizing Contribution

OpTek Corporation
Variable Costing Income Statement

Product	Qty.	Revenue	Variable Cost	Contribution
Axle housings	160	$6,800	$3,200	$3,600
Wheel hubs	240	8,400	4,200	4,200
Totals	400	$15,200	$7,400	$7,800
		Less monthly fixed cost		5,000
		Net operating profit		$2,800

They were all amazed. They reviewed the results very carefully and methodically:

1. The resulting product mix did in fact produce the highest monthly net operating profit, which was: (a) 40 percent higher than the next closest option of cost minimization ($2,800 ÷ $2,000 = 1.4 = 40% increase); (b) 63 percent higher than with their present strategy of producing an equal number of each part ($2,800 ÷ $1,720 = 1.63 = 63% increase).
2. The resulting product mix did *not* produce the highest revenue compared with the other strategies.
3. The resulting product mix did *not* produce the lowest variable cost compared with the other strategies.
4. The resulting product mix *did*, however, produce the highest contribution, i.e., distance between revenue and variable cost.

   Upon examining this fact they came to this realization: *The objective that maximizes contribution will always maximize net operating profit and provide the lowest break-even level.*
5. The resulting plant utilization was definitely **not** the highest compared to the other strategies.

$$\frac{1{,}000 \text{ available processing hours} - \text{slack } (120 + 64 + 104)}{1{,}000 \text{ available processing hours}} = 71.2\%$$

6. They considered further that the product mix included 240 wheel hubs. That represented 60 percent of the total mix. Wheel hubs, however, did not have the highest individual part contribution.

Product	Contribution Each
Axle housing	$22.50
Brake caliper	19.00
Wheel hub	**17.50**
Valve body	15.00
Differential case	10.00

The brake caliper has the second highest part contribution, and yet there are none of them in the contribution maximizing mix. The answer lies in the fact that brake calipers require too much work-center time, which couldn't justify their production. In other words, even though their individual contribution was higher than wheel hubs, OpTek couldn't make a sufficient number of them to maximize total facility contribution. There was no other mix of products that OpTek could make that would generate more profit than:

<u>160 Axle housings</u>
<u>240 Wheel hubs</u>
400

They also noted that two constraints surfaced with this optimum product mix, i.e., core and molding per Table 4.14.

Summarizing the Results

Mr. Porter asked Jim to prepare a summary page listing each of the strategies that they had evaluated and rank them in order of their profitability. This summary is presented as Table 4.16.

OpTek Corporation

Operational Strategies   *Ranked by Profits Generated*

Strategy	Revenue	Throughput	Variable Cost	Utilization	Contribution	Net Profit	Ranking
Maximize contribution	$15,200	$12,880	$7,400	71.2%	$7,800	$2,800	1
Minimize variable cost	$14,000	$11,200	$7,000	52.0%	$7,000	$2,000	2
Maximize revenue	$16,040	$14,656	$9,080	82.2%	$6,960	$1,960	3
Maximize throughput	$15,998	$14,708	$9,230	83.1%	$6,768	$1,768	4
Maintain status quo	$15,000	$12,600	$8,280	82.4%	$6,720	$1,720	5
Maximize utilization	$14,670	$11,925	$8,695	90.6%	$5,975	$ 975	6

Perhaps the single biggest surprise to OpTek's staff when reviewing Table 4.16 was that *the strategy that produced the highest total plant utilization of 90.6 percent also generated the lowest profit.* In addition, compared to maintaining status quo, i.e., changing nothing, OpTek could increase its net operating profit by 63 percent by simply changing its product mix.

Measuring the Improvement of OpTek's Financial Performance

Jim then calculated their primary financial performance statistics provided by the strategy of contribution maximization:

Monthly net operating profit = $2,800 × 12 = $33,600 annualized profit

$$\frac{\text{Capital}}{\text{productivity}} = \frac{\text{Ending assets}}{\text{Beginning assets}} = \frac{\text{Output}}{\text{Input}} = \frac{\$433,600}{\$400,000} = 1.084$$

$$\text{ROI} = \frac{\text{Ending assets} - \text{beginning assets}}{\text{Beginning assets}} = \frac{\text{Profit}}{\text{Beginning assets}} = \frac{\$33,600}{\$400,000} = 8.4\%$$

Break-Even Level

OpTek's break-even level would also improve substantially:

$$\frac{\$7,800 \text{ monthly contribution (per Table 4.16)}}{400 \text{ total molds made}} = \$19.50 \text{ contribution per mold}$$

$$\frac{\$5,000 \text{ total monthly fixed cost}}{\$19.50 \text{ contribution per mold}} = 256 \text{ molds to break even}$$

$$\frac{256 \text{ molds to break even}}{400 \text{ total available molds}} = 64\% \text{ of molding capacity to break even}$$

Mr. Porter was becoming more optimistic as he compared their potential financial position to that which existed before they had learned of optimization technology:

1. ROI would increase from 5.1 percent to 8.4 percent
2. OpTek's break-even level would improve from 74.5 percent of molding capacity to 64 percent.

He felt that they were definitely on the way to learning how to manage their business. Then Mr. Porter addressed his staff philosophically as if he were a university professor.

"One of the greatest problems in our industrial sector today is that *a large percentage of manufacturers are producing a sub-optimal product mix.* The argument has recently been presented that many of us were involved in counterproductive practices such as focusing on overhead absorption or concentrating on maximizing gross profit, and now it is evident that many of us are also producing a sub-optimal product mix.

"There will be those who will say that our optimum product mix consisting of 160 axle housings and 240 wheel hubs may not be possible, or feasible, due to, say, market constraints. Perhaps this is true. The fact remains, however, that the contribution opportunity for us is $7,800 per month with this mix of products.

"*Every plant should be able to define the product mix that maximizes its profit opportunity and must realize that any other mix will produce less profit.* Choosing to produce another mix will, in essence, 'manage down' our profit level. Every manager should be aware of the cost of making a sub-optimal product mix.

"We at OpTek now have a good idea of the benefits of optimization technology. For sure, we have learned how wrong it is to make product decisions in isolation."

Summary—Key Points

Several significant issues were made clear in this chapter:

- The analysis of the financial performance statistics of a plant—the productivity of capital/ROI and the break-even level—is an expression of the success of optimization techniques.
- There are many different department profit-enhancing theories within a plant, but the manager has to consider the plant as a whole.
- Revenue, cost, plant utilization and throughput were previously considered to be primary factors when calculating profitability.
- Product decisions cannot be made on the basis of an individual part's price/cost relationship.
- Maximizing total plant contribution will automatically maximize that plant's total net operating profit.
- A plant now has the means to measure the cost of producing any product mix other than the mix determined using optimization techniques. The difference in contribution between the mix determined with optimization techniques and the contribution resulting from any other scenario is the cost of producing the nonoptimizing product mix.

To conclude: No product decision should be made in isolation; all factors should be considered.

Getting the Most from What You Have: Learning How to Manage with Optimization Techniques

CHAPTER 5

Measuring the Financial Benefits of Manufacturing Process Improvements

Having discovered that contribution maximization is the profit maximizing strategy, any suggested operational change can be evaluated financially by comparing the total plant contribution before the change with the simulated contribution incorporating the change. Specifically for OpTek its benchmark would be the $7,800 monthly contribution with its present product choices, departmental capacities, and product routings. In this chapter, OpTek will use its newfound methodology to measure the financial impact of manufacturing process improvements.

Chapter Contents

- The benchmark from which to measure the impact of proposed manufacturing activities
- Process improvements should focus on production constraints
- Optimization techniques provide unpredictable results
- Estimating the potential impact of process improvements
- Optimization technology far surpasses traditional wisdom, including intuition

The Benchmark from Which to Measure the Impact of Proposed Manufacturing Activities

OpTek has discovered the operating objective that generated the most profit, i.e., *the maximization of contribution*. From this point on it will measure the financial benefits provided with any proposed manufacturing activity in terms of *incremental contribution*. So as they consider making process improvements in their plant, they will measure the projected financial benefits resulting from such improvements relative to their newly discovered benchmark, which is a plant contribution of $7,800 per month. They remember Table 4.14, which is reproduced below as Table 5.1.

Table 5.1 OpTek's Benchmark Product Mix for Contribution Maximization

Objective: **Maximize Contribution**					
Product	Qty.	Department	Hrs. Required	Slack	Opportunity
Valve bodies	0	Core	200	0	$10.00
Axle housings	160	Assembly	80	120	0
Differential cases	0	Molding	200	0	29.00
Wheel hubs	240	Cleaning	136	64	0
Brake calipers	0	Grinding	96	104	0
Totals	400		712	288	
Maximum contribution possible $7,800					

Process Improvements Should Focus on Production Constraints

As the staff viewed Table 5.1 they noted that two constraints were present when contribution was maximized, i.e., core and molding, while slack existed in assembly, cleaning, and grinding.

One of OpTek's manufacturing engineers, Ben, has been working on improving the core process for several products. His efforts intensified now that core was in fact a constraint. Also noting that the wheel hubs made up 60 percent of the optimum mix, he concentrated his efforts on this part in the core process. Ben stated that he was confident that he could actually eliminate the core process on the wheel hub. The next step was to measure the financial benefit associated with this proposed improvement.

When using optimization techniques, the beginning point is the product routing matrix originally presented as Table 2.4 (pg. 16) and reproduced here as Table 5.2.

Table 5.2 Product Routing Matrix for OpTek Corporation

	Product					
Department	Valve Body	Axle Housing	Differential Case	Wheel Hub	Brake Caliper	**Time Available**
Core	.4	.8	.1	.3	.9	200 hrs.
Assembly	.7	.2	.1	.2	.7	200 hrs.
Molding	.5	.5	.5	.5	.5	200 hrs.
Cleaning	.1	.7	.2	.1	.6	200 hrs.
Grinding	.3	.3	.1	.2	.8	200 hrs.

If the core process time for the wheel hub can be eliminated, the routing matrix must incorporate this change, and the core work center would then look like this:

Department	Valve Body	Axle Housing	Differential Case	Wheel Hub	Brake Caliper	**Time Available**
Core	.4	.8	.1	0	.9	200 hrs.

The hourly labor rate at OpTek was $10.00, so the variable cost of the wheel hub would be reduced by $3.00. This $3.00 reduction in variable cost would likewise increase the wheel hub's contribution by the same $3.00. The proposed contribution for the wheel hub would then be **$20.50** ($17.50 + $3.00 = $20.50).

Now the financial benefits made possible by eliminating the core operation on the wheel hub can be measured. The initial reaction would be that the contribution would increase by $720 (240 = quantity of wheel hubs in the optimum mix × $3.00 = $720). However, *with optimization technology, the benefit will nearly always be more than that expected with traditional means.* The problem is input to the OpTek Algorithm with contribution maximization as the objective:

> **Maximize $15.00(valve body) + $22.50(axle housing) + $10.00(differential cases) + $20.50(wheel hub) + $19.00(brake calipers)**

(Subject to the product routings and departmental capacities in Table 2.4 with the changes noted above, i.e., core time is 0 for the wheel hub, and its contribution has been increased to $20.50, as noted.)

Table 5.3 OpTek's Proposed Contribution with the Elimination of the Core Operation on the Wheel Hub

Objective: **Maximize Contribution**					
Product	Qty.	Department	Hrs. Required	Slack	Opportunity
Valve bodies	0	Core	200	0	$ 2.50
Axle housings	250	Assembly	80	120	0
Differential cases	0	Molding	200	0	$41.00
Wheel hubs	150	Cleaning	190	10	0
Brake calipers	0	Grinding	105	95	0
Totals	400		775	225	
Maximum contribution possible $8,700					

There is no need to present Table 5.3 in income statement format, inasmuch as fixed cost will remain the same. So any change in contribution will reflect directly in net operating profit.

Optimization Techniques Provide Unpredictable Results

The results of Table 5.3 require careful analysis:

1. There is a substantial increase in contribution, from $7,800 to $8,700.
2. The same two products appear in Table 5.3, and the benchmark mix as illustrated in Table 5.1 but in a substantially different ratio.
3. Even though the core operation was eliminated for the wheel hub, the number of wheel hubs in the new mix decreased. The reason for this phenomenon is that the contribution for each wheel hub, even after the process improvement, is $20.50, which is still less than the $22.50 for each axle housing. The time made available by the core process improvement on the wheel hub was better utilized by producing more axle housings. "Better utilized" means generating more contribution. Even Mr. Porter wasn't prepared for this result.

Estimating the Potential Impact of Process Improvements

They were very pleased with the results of this initial simulation. Stephanie reminded them, however, that they had two constraints that presented opportunities for process improvements. According to their benchmark mix in Table 5.1, molding was also constrained with their optimum product mix. They also noted that the opportunity associated with molding was higher than the opportunity for core.

Department	Opportunity per Table 5.1
Core	$10.00
Molding	$29.00

The molding unit was machine paced. The opportunity to improve the molding process would be in the reduction of the cycle time for the molding machine. If a reduction of the molding machine cycle time was possible then all products could benefit by such an improvement. Considering that the molding operation was machine paced, the wages paid to the labor crew on the molding line was considered to be fixed. Therefore, any reduction in the molding machine's cycle time would not affect a part's variable cost or its contribution.

Ben came through again. After a great deal of effort, he was able to reduce the molding machine's cycle time from .5 hours to .4 hours. To be quite truthful, OpTek's staff didn't really have a clue as to how to measure the financial benefit provided from this process change. They weren't even sure that there would be a financial benefit associated with this improvement because there would be no change in part contributions. Before they simulated this scenario, they set the core process time required on the wheel hub back to .3 hours and its contribution back to the original $17.50. This would ensure that any change in plant contribution would be identified with the molding machine cycle-time reduction.

Jim noted that they could end the speculation by activating the OpTek Algorithm, with contribution maximization as the objective. First, however, the routing matrix needed to reflect the reduction in molding's cycle time.

Table 5.4 OpTek's Routing Matrix Revised to Reflect the Improvement in Cycle Time of the Molding Unit

	Product					
Department	Valve Body	Axle Housing	Differential Case	Wheel Hub	Brake Caliper	Time Available
Core	.4	.8	.1	.3	.9	200 hrs.
Assembly	.7	.2	.1	.2	.7	200 hrs.
Molding	.4	.4	.4	.4	.4	200 hrs.
Cleaning	.1	.7	.2	.1	.6	200 hrs.
Grinding	.3	.3	.1	.2	.8	200 hrs.

The objective to maximize contribution is then:

Maximize $15.00(valve body) + $22.50(axle housing) + $10.00(differential case) + $17.50(wheel hub) + $19.00(brake caliper)

(Subject to the product routings and departmental capacities in Table 2.4 with the change for the molding work center noted in Table 5.4.)

Table 5.5 Product Mix and Maximum Contribution Possible by Reducing Molding's Cycle Time from .5 Hours to .4 Hours.

Objective: **Maximize Contribution**					
Product	**Qty.**	**Department**	**Hrs. Required**	**Slack**	**Opportunity**
Valve bodies	0	Core	200	0	$10.00
Axle housings	100	Assembly	100	100	0
Differential cases	0	Molding	200	0	36.25
Wheel hubs	400	Cleaning	110	90	0
Brake calipers	0	Grinding	110	90	0
Totals	**500**		**720**	**280**	
Maximum contribution possible $9,250					

Once again, the staff studied the results carefully:

1. The contribution increased substantially, from $7,800 to $9,250. This improvement exceeded the financial benefit derived from eliminating the core operation on the wheel hub illustrated in Table 5.3.
2. This present scenario still includes just the two parts, i.e., axle housings and wheel hubs, but in a substantially different ratio. Now the mix includes 80 percent wheel hubs and 20 percent axle housings even though axle housings have a substantially higher contribution per part. The benchmark mix included just 40 percent axle housings and 60 percent wheel hubs.
3. The reduction of molding cycle time allows for more total parts/molds to be made, from 400 to 500.

$$\frac{200 \text{ hours available molding time}}{.4 \text{ hours per part/mold}} = 500 \text{ parts/molds}$$

Optimization Technology Far Surpasses Traditional Wisdom, Including Intuition

OpTek's management was learning things that they could never have learned within the confines of traditional thinking. They were elated with the information provided with optimization technology using the OpTek Algorithm. Jim prepared an analysis comparing the increased contribution achieved with the core process improvement on the wheel hub, with the increased contribution realized with the improvement in the cycle time on the molding machine.

Increased contribution from
core process change on wheel hub
$8,700 less benchmark contribution $7,800   = $ 900

Increased contribution from
improving molding cycle time
$9,250 less benchmark contribution $7,800   = $1,450

Combined financial benefit $2,350

After reviewing the simulated results, they decided that both process improvements were well worth the effort, so they instructed Ben to incorporate the change to eliminate the core operation on the wheel hub and to proceed to improve the molding unit's cycle time from .5 hours to .4 hours. They also expected to confirm the $2,350 per month financial benefit from these two actions. The routing matrix was modified to reflect both improvements as follows:

Table 5.6 Revised Routing Matrix Reflecting Process Improvements to Both Core and Molding

Department	Product					Time Available
	Valve Body	Axle Housing	Differential Case	Wheel Hub	Brake Caliper	
Core	.4	.8	.1	0	.9	200 hrs.
Assembly	.7	.2	.1	.2	.7	200 hrs.
Molding	.4	.4	.4	.4	.4	200 hrs.
Cleaning	.1	.7	.2	.1	.6	200 hrs.
Grinding	.3	.3	.1	.2	.8	200 hrs.

So once again they activated the OpTek Algorithm with the objective of maximizing contribution.

Maximize $15.00(valve body) + $22.50(axle housing) + $10.00(differential case) + $20.50(wheel hub) + $19.00(brake caliper)

(Subject to product routings and departmental capacities in Table 2.4 and the changes noted in Table 5.6.)

Table 5.7 Projected Contribution When Two Process Improvements Are Done
Simultaneously

Objective: **Maximize Contribution**					
Product	**Qty.**	**Department**	**Hrs. Required**	**Slack**	**Opportunity**
Valve bodies	0	Core	200	0	$2.50
Axle housings	250	Assembly	100	100	0
Differential cases	0	Molding	200	0	$51.25
Wheel Hubs	250	Cleaning	200	0	0
Brake calipers	0	Grinding	125	75	0
Totals	**500**		**825**	**175**	
Maximum contribution possible $10,750					

Immediately, Mr. Porter and the others noticed that the incremental contribution from incorporating both process changes simultaneously exceeded the projected contribution increase when these two process changes were considered individually.

Table 5.8 Comparison of Contribution When Incorporating Process Changes
Simultaneously vs. Separately

Increased contribution from incorporating process changes individually: ($900 from core process improvement on wheel hubs + $1,450 from improving molding cycle time)	= $2,350
Increased contribution from incorporating both process improvements simultaneously: ($10,750 less benchmark contribution $7,800)	= $2,950
Additional contribution by incorporating both process changes simultaneously	= $ 600

As the staff reviewed the results they came to the conclusion that there is potential and, likely, *synergy* involved when making multiple changes to the data set simultaneously. The above results, once again, would never have been considered without the aid of optimization technology. All of them were extremely pleased with what they were learning. They were very anxious to apply this new tool to another very important issue, i.e., analysis of the make-or-buy decision.

Summary—Key Points

This chapter illustrates new opportunities, not previously available when using traditional wisdom and intuition. The key points are as follows:

- It is important to establish a benchmark from which to measure the impact of proposed manufacturing activities.
- In the past, if a process improvement was made on a certain product, the financial benefit would be confined to that product.
- Optimization techniques, however, refute that logic. The optimal solution affecting the total plant's profit is found by transcending individual product statistics. Process improvements should focus on production constraints.
- If multiple constraints exist in a production facility, relief to just one of them will favorably effect total plant contribution.

This chapter also introduces the synergistic affect on profitability when multiple improvements are made simultaneously that affect routings, capacities, or product contributions.

CHAPTER 6

A New Look at the Make-or-Buy Decision

This chapter will introduce optimization techniques to the make-or-buy decision process.

OpTek felt that there were major opportunities to improve total plant profit with selective outsourcing. Up to this point, however, it had made such decisions based on comparing an individual part's total standard cost to make it in house with a vendor's proposed price to supply it to them.

Chapter Contents

- All products should be potential candidates for the make-or-buy decision
- Outsourcing decisions cannot be made on the basis of an individual part's price/cost relationship
- Any restriction that limits the freedom of the optimization algorithm will reduce contribution
- Outsourcing decisions must be viewed holistically
- Product mix changes present a marketing consideration
- One plant's trash may be another plant's treasure
- Outsourcing should be a win–win scenario

Stephanie had recently completed a class at the local university entitled "Vendor Outsourcing Strategy." She thought that perhaps optimization technology could be used to help OpTek better identify those jobs that would be viable outsourcing candidates vs. those that should be kept in house. The starting point in their analyses would once again be their benchmark product mix, presented here as Table 6.1

Table 6.1 OpTek's Benchmark Product Mix for Contribution Maximization

Objective: **Maximize Contribution**					
Product	**Qty.**	**Department**	**Hrs. Required**	**Slack**	**Opportunity**
Valve bodies	0	Core	200	0	$10.00
Axle housings	160	Assembly	80	120	0
Differential cases	0	Molding	200	0	29.00
Wheel hubs	240	Cleaning	136	64	0
Brake calipers	0	Grinding	96	104	0
Totals	**400**		**712**	**288**	
Maximum contribution possible $7,800					

OpTek had recently entered into contracts with its customers guaranteeing to supply them with 160 axle housings and 240 wheel hubs each month.

All Products Should Be Potential Candidates for the Make-or-Buy Decision

Even with its contractual obligations, OpTek was evaluating two proposals from a local vender, Crow-Bar Enterprises. OpTek was considering outsourcing some of its two primary products, i.e., axle housings and wheel hubs. OpTek knew that if it did this, it would need to produce something else in their place to utilize the molding capacity of 400 per month. The truth was that they really didn't know how to evaluate Crow-Bar's proposals.

Proposal 1
Crow-Bar Enterprises proposes to provide axle housings to
OpTekCorporation in accordance with the following terms:

Product	Qty.	Price
Axle housing	100	$35.00 each

With this proposal, OpTek would be required to make at least 60 axle housings and 240 wheel hubs to satisfy their contractual obligations to its customers. In the decision process, it reviewed the axle housing's total standard cost from Table 2.2 (p. 14).

Variable cost	$20.00
Allocated fixed cost	12.50
Total standard cost	**$32.50**

Outsourcing Decisions Cannot Be Made on the Basis of an Individual Part's Price/Cost Relationship

At this point, Jim quickly dismissed the proposal inasmuch as Crow-Bar's proposed price of $35.00 was $2.50 more than OpTek's total standard cost to make the part, which even included allocated overhead. Mr. Porter cautioned Jim to slow down: "You're still thinking in terms of the standard cost system. Let's evaluate this proposal using optimization techniques."

So they turned the proposal over to the OpTek Algorithm, again with the objective to maximize contribution. They would compare the newly determined contribution with the $7,800 benchmark amount. The difference would be the financial impact related to outsourcing the 100 axle housings:

Maximize $15.00(valve body) + $22.50(axle housing) + $10.00(differential case) + $17.50(wheel hub) + $19.00(brake caliper)

(Subject to the product routings and departmental capacities in Table 2.4 [p. 16].)

They also had to limit the quantity of axle housings to be made in-house at 60:

Axle housings = 60

Table 6.2 Maximum Internal Contribution When Outsourcing 100 Axle Housings

Objective: **Maximize Contribution**					
Product	Qty.	Department	Hrs. Required	Slack	Opportunity
Valve bodies	0	Core	200.00	0	$ 2.50
Axle housings	60	Assembly	121.67	78.33	0
Differential cases	0	Molding	200.00	0	33.50
Wheel hubs	257	Cleaning	117.67	82.33	0
Brake calipers	83	Grinding	136.00	64.00	0
Totals	400		775.34	224.66	
Maximum contribution possible $7,425					

Any Restriction That Limits the Freedom of the Optimization Algorithm Will Reduce Contribution

It was immediately noted that OpTek's *internal contribution had decreased substantially*, from $7,800 to $7,425. Of course, this just confirmed Jim's suspicions, and in fact he commented that the results were just as he had expected.

They also noted that in addition to the 60 axle housings in the mix there were also 17 additional wheel hubs (257 now – 240 original benchmark) + 83 brake calipers. The 17 + 83 = the 100 new parts to replace the 100 axle housings that Crow-Bar had proposed to make per Proposal 1. Reuben assured them that selling the 17 additional wheel hubs and 83 brake calipers would not present a problem.

Outsourcing Decisions Must Be Viewed Holistically

Mr. Porter wasn't discouraged yet, as he instructed Jim to present Table 6.2 in the variable costing income statement format along with the transaction of the 100 axle housings being considered for outsourcing to Crow-Bar. See Table 6.3.

Mr. Porter explained that the $750 profit on the 100 axle housing transaction with Crow-Bar could indeed be considered an incremental contribution, because the $35.00 cost each to OpTek became OpTek's variable cost.

Of particular interest to Jim was the fact that the only cost avoided with the outsourcing transaction with Crow-Bar was OpTek's variable cost to make them in-house. None of the $5,000 monthly fixed cost was avoided, and yet total profit improved.

They all found it to be very interesting that *they could outsource a job for more than its total standard cost and still increase their total plant profits.*

Table 6.3 OpTek's Proposed Monthly Net Operating Profit When Outsourcing 100 Axle Housings to Crow-Bar

OpTek Corporation

Variable Costing Income Statement

Internal contribution from Table 6.2		$7,425
Revenue from sale of 100 axle housings at $42.50 each, outsourced to Crow-Bar	$4,250	
Cost to outsource 100 axle housings to Crow-Bar quoted at $35.00 each	3,500	
Incremental contribution from outsourcing activity		$ 750
OpTek's adjusted contribution		$8,175
Less monthly fixed cost		5,000
Net operating profit		$3,175

Crow-Bar had submitted two proposals so they began to evaluate the second one.

Proposal 2

Crow-Bar Enterprises proposes to provide wheel hubs to OpTek Corporation in accordance with the following terms:

Product	Qty.	Price
Wheel hubs	**200**	**$25.00 each**

With this proposal, OpTek would be required to make the remaining 40 wheel hubs and at least 160 axle housings to satisfy its contractual obligations to its customers. Optek reviewed the wheel hub's total standard cost from Table 2.2.

Variable cost	$17.50
Allocated fixed cost	6.50
Total standard cost	$24.00

Once again OpTek's total standard cost for the wheel hub was less than the cost that Crow-Bar had quoted to make it. However, Jim held his peace this time.

It was time for the OpTek Algorithm to go to work and again they would compare the newly determined contribution with the benchmark amount of $7,800 so that any difference could be attributable exclusively to the wheel hub transaction:

Maximize $15.00(valve body) + $22.50(axle housing) + $10.00(differential case) + $17.50(wheel hub) + $19.00(brake caliper)

(Subject to product routings and departmental capacities in Table 2.4).

The one addition was:

Wheel hubs = 40

Table 6.4 Product Mix That Maximizes Contribution When Outsourcing 200 Wheel Hubs to Crow-Bar Enterprises

Objective: **Maximize Contribution**					
Product	Qty.	Department	Hrs. Required	Slack	Opportunity
Valve bodies	0	Core	200.00	0	$17.85
Axle housings	217	Assembly	65.72	134.28	0
Differential cases	143	Molding	200.00	0	16.42
Wheel hubs	40	Cleaning	184.58	15.42	0
Brake calipers	0	Grinding	87.43	112.57	0
Totals	400		737.73	262.27	
Maximum contribution possible $7,014					

They quickly noticed that the contribution had decreased not only from the benchmark of $7,800 but also from the $7,425 when the axle housings were being considered for outsourcing, per Table 6.2. Logic caused them to realize that whenever the output of the algorithm is overridden, as in the case of forcing the product mix to include just 40 wheel hubs instead of the 240 selected per the optimum mix, OpTek's internal contribution would automatically decrease. The next step was to present Table 6.4, along with the 200 wheel hub transaction with Crow-Bar, in the variable costing income statement format.

Product Mix Changes Present a Marketing Consideration

Reuben once again reviewed Table 6.4 to see if the 200 parts chosen by the algorithm to replace the 200 wheel hubs outsourced to Crow-Bar would present a marketing problem. He confirmed that the additional 57 axle housings plus the 143 differential cases would be no problem to sell at current prices. If, however, Reuben had indicated that the market would only accept 120 differential cases, a further addition to the data set limiting differential cases to 120 would be required. This action would automatically reduce internal contribution and most likely alter the

Table 6.5 OpTek's Proposed Monthly Net Operating Profit Considering the Outsourcing of 200 Wheel Hubs to Crow-Bar

OpTek Corporation

Variable-Costing Income Statement

Internal contribution from Table 6.4		$7,014
Revenue from sale of 200 wheel hubs at $35.00 each, outsourced to Crow-Bar	$7,000	
Cost to outsource 200 wheel hubs to Crow-Bar quoted at $25.00 each	5,000	
Incremental contribution from outsourcing activity		$2,000
OpTek's adjusted contribution		$9,014
Less monthly fixed cost		5,000
Net operating profit		$4,014

mix. However, without activating the algorithm, the final result of this action is unknown. The algorithm can, however, accommodate any such scenario.

OpTek's management was really amazed at the results produced by using optimization techniques. It appeared that the more they outsourced, the more net operating profit they realized.

One Plant's Trash May Be Another Plant's Treasure

Everything was looking up for OpTek when the strangest thing happened. The general manager of Crow-Bar called Mr. Porter and said: "We're really happy with our business relationship and in fact would like to increase our participation with you. We would, however, like to submit an alternative proposal for your consideration to replace our previous Proposals 1 and 2. Now I don't want to appear to be boasting, but we have developed a model that tells us what type of work fits best in our plant. We call it the *Crow-Bar Do Loop*. As you know, we have different equipment than you and our process is slightly different than yours. Anyway, to make a long story short, we propose to make 100 of your valve bodies and 200 of your brake calipers instead of the axle housings or wheel hubs. We don't know your cost to make them, but because they fit our plant so well, we propose a price of $30.00 each for either the valve bodies or brake calipers. Take a look at it and give me a call. If you have any interest we will submit a formal quote."

Mr. Porter thanked him for the proposal and called his staff in to review it with them. They began by examining their benchmark mix in Table 6.1 and noted that neither the valve body or the brake caliper was included in their plant's optimum mix. In other words these two parts were not a good fit for OpTek's plant but appeared to be a good fit for Crow-Bar's operation.

In addition, Crow-Bar's quote for both the valve body and brake caliper was less than OpTek's total standard cost for them:

Product	Variable Cost	Allocated Fixed Cost	Total Standard Cost	20% Markup	Difference
Valve body	$25.00	$10.00	$35.00	$30.00	($5.00)
Brake caliper	21.00	17.50	38.50	30.00	($8.50)

Before they proceeded, Mr. Porter asked Reuben if he could sell these additional products. Reuben said that he could get an immediate contract for them if they could reduce the prices to $38.00 instead of the present price of $40.00 each per Table 2.2. Jim then prepared a pro forma income statement to summarize the results of this proposal.

Table 6.6 OpTek's Net Operating Profit With Original Benchmark Mix Plus Outsourcing 100 Valve Bodies and 200 Brake Calipers to Crow-Bar

OpTek Corporation

Variable-Costing Income Statement

Internal Contribution from Table 6.1		$ 7,800
Revenue from the sale of 100 valve bodies: 100 × $38.00	$3,800	
Variable cost of 100 valve bodies: 100 × $30.00	3,000	
Additional contribution from valve body transaction		$ 800
Revenue from sale of 200 brake calipers: 200 × $38.00	$7,600	
Variable cost of 200 brake calipers: 200 × $30.00	$6,000	
Additional contribution from brake cylinder transaction		$ 1,600
Total facility contribution		10,200
Less monthly fixed cost		5,000
Net operating profit		$ 5,200

This looked too good to be true. They decided to calculate their projected ROI with this latest opportunity:

$$\text{ROI:} \frac{\text{Ending assets} - \text{beginning assets}}{\text{Beginning assets}} = \frac{\text{Profit}}{\text{Beginning assets}} = \frac{\$62,400^*}{\$400,000} = 15.6\%$$

*$5,200 monthly profit from Table 6.6 × 12 = annualized profit.

Outsourcing Should Be a Win–Win Scenario

Upon completing the evaluation of Crow-Bar's proposal Mr. Porter called Crow-Bar's general manager: "We have carefully considered your proposal and have decided to accept it. I don't know much about your so-called Crow-Bar Do Loop, but if in fact it tells you which type of work fits best in your plant to maximize your profits, then you have a definite competitive advantage. Congratulations."

He hung up the phone and swiveled around in his chair with a slight grin as if he had just negotiated the contract of the century.

Summary—Key Points

Certain points were discussed in this chapter:

- The make-or-buy decision should be made for all products without exception.
- A part's price/cost relationship cannot be the reason an outsourcing decision is made.
- Whenever the freedom of the algorithm is overridden, the result will be a decrease in the objective function value.
- Each plant within a given industry has its own unique capabilities, based on its specific processes that makes one product financially desirable to one plant but not to another.

Perhaps the most startling discovery in this chapter is:

- A plant may be able to outsource products in its existing optimum product mix at a cost that exceeds its total standard cost to make them in house, and still increase total plant profits.

CHAPTER 7

How to Evaluate New Business with Optimization Techniques

This chapter will examine another daily business challenge, i.e., the fear of losing business. Optimization techniques will be used to measure the cost of losing specific business as well as how to choose the optimal replacement business.

This chapter will also clearly illustrate that traditional thinking linked with existing standard cost systems will provide very misleading information relative both to measuring the financial impact of lost business as well as the ability to evaluate the financial merits of replacement business.

Chapter Contents

- Measuring the financial impact of lost business
- Doing the right thing in a very wrong way
- Optimization techniques do not mix well with traditional thinking
- Optimization techniques should prompt the rethinking of opportunities that were previously rejected with traditional wisdom

OpTek's marketing manager, Reuben, was reading an article about a forecasted slowdown in the transportation industry. His initial reaction was that this slowdown might affect the sale of wheel hubs. In fact, it caused him to consider the possibility of losing their contract to supply 240 wheel hubs monthly.

Measuring the Financial Impact of Lost Business

He relayed his concern to Mr. Porter, who in turn asked him what the financial consequence would be if they lost the wheel hub business. The starting point in Reuben's analysis was their benchmark mix, reproduced here as Table 7.1.

Table 7.1 OpTek's Benchmark Product Mix for Contribution Maximization

Objective: **Maximize Contribution**					
Product	Qty.	Department	Hrs. Required	Slack	Opportunity
Valve bodies	0	Core	200	0	$10.00
Axle housings	160	Assembly	80	120	0
Differential cases	0	Molding	200	0	29.00
Wheel hubs	240	Cleaning	136	64	0
Brake calipers	0	Grinding	96	104	0
Totals	400		712	288	
Maximum contribution possible $7,800					

Reuben's first thought was that their profit would decrease by $4,200 (240 each × contribution each of $17.50). He caught himself, however, before telling that to Mr. Porter because he realized that the OpTek Algorithm would define a new product mix to utilize the 240 molds now being used for wheel hubs. He did realize that profits would in fact be less inasmuch as the algorithm had already provided the maximum contribution with the available parts that included the wheel hubs. He remembered that any time one of the parameters of the data set is restricted the resulting objective function value, in the present case contribution, would be less than without the restrictions. So Reuben did the proper thing. He activated the algorithm with one addition, i.e.,

Wheel hubs = 0

He then proceeded to determine the maximum contribution without wheel hubs.

Maximize $15.00 (valve body) + $22.50 (axle housing) + $10.00 (differential case)
+ $17.50 (wheel hub) + $19.00 (brake caliper)

(Subject to product routings and departmental capacities per Table 2.4 [p. 16].)

Table 7.2 OpTek's Projected Monthly Contribution Without Wheel Hubs

Objective: **Maximize Contribution**					
Product	**Qty.**	**Department**	**Hrs. Required**	**Slack**	**Opportunity**
Valve bodies	0	Core	200.00	0	$17.85
Axle housings	229	Assembly	62.86	137.14	0
Differential cases	171	Molding	200.00	0	16.42
Wheel hubs	0	Cleaning	194.29	5.71	0
Brake calipers	0	Grinding	85.72	114.28	0
Totals	400		742.87	257.13	
Maximum contribution possible $6,862					

At this point Reuben could report to Mr. Porter that the loss of the wheel hub business would cost OpTek $938 per month.

Benchmark contribution = $7,800 – $6,862 contribution without wheel hubs = $938

Mr. Porter then asked the next logical question: "Is there other work available to compensate for the possible loss of the wheel hub business?"

Doing the Right Thing in a Very Wrong Way

Reuben was ready for that question and replied that there were, in fact, three new jobs with a request for a quote in his office. He was told to evaluate them and get back with his recommendations. The proposed routings for the three prospective jobs are summarized in Table 7.3.

Table 7.3 Routing Matrix for Three Prospective Jobs to be Quoted

Department	Gearbox	Counterweight	Tie Rod
Core	.3	0	.3
Assembly	.2	0	.4
Molding	5	.5	.25
Cleaning	.3	.4	.5
Grinding	.5	.2	.5

Examination of these jobs revealed that the counterweight was a solid part that didn't require core or assembly. The tie rod was a long and narrow part that could be molded with two in each mold.

Jim provided the variable cost figures to Reuben, and then Reuben assigned the contribution for each part based on marketing data for the selling prices.

Table 7.4 Determination of Individual Part Contributions for Three Prospective Jobs

	Gearbox	Counterweight	Tie Rod
Selling price	$37.50	$29.50	$38.50
Variable cost	20.50	14.00	24.50
Contribution	$17.00	$15.50	$14.00

Jim and Reuben were in total agreement that the best choice to replace the wheel hub would be the gearbox. They were really proud that the subject of allocated overhead never came up as they evaluated these prospective parts. The next

Table 7.5 Capacity Analysis to Determine if OpTek Could Produce 240 Gearboxes in Place of 240 Wheel Hubs

OpTek Corporation

Capacity Analysis for Gearbox

Department	A	B	C = A + B	D	E = C – D
Core	0	72	72	72	0
Assembly	120	48	168	48	120
Molding	0	120	120	120	0
Cleaning	64	24	88	72	16
Grinding	104	48	152	120	32

Column legend:

A = Present slack with wheel hubs from Table 7.1.

B = Departmental time made available without producing wheel hubs, (240 wheel hubs × routing from Table 2.4):

240 × .3 = 72
240 × .2 = 48
240 × .5 = 120
240 × .1 = 24
240 × .2 = 48

C = Capacity available for the gearbox.

D = Capacity required to produce 240 gearboxes, (240 Gearboxes × routing from Table 7.3):

240 × .3 = 72
240 × .2 = 48
240 × .5 = 120
240 × .3 = 72
240 × .5 = 120

E = Slack and/or constraint.

step was to ensure that the plant had the capacity to produce the gearbox. They enlisted Stephanie's help for this task. She came through with flying colors and provided the capacity analysis as requested (Table 7.5).

It was in fact determined that OpTek's facility could produce 240 gearboxes instead of 240 wheel hubs plus the required 160 axle housings. Before they made their presentation to Mr. Porter, Jim drafted a variable costing income statement reflecting the inclusion of the gearboxes in place of the wheel hubs.

Table 7.6 OpTek's Income Statement Reflecting 240 Gearboxes Replacing 240 Wheel Hubs

OpTek Corporation
Variable Costing Income Statement

Product	Qty.	Revenue	Variable Cost	Contribution
Axle housings	160	$ 6,800	$3,200	$3,600
Gearboxes	240	$ 9,000	$4,900	$4,080
Totals	400	$15,800	$8,120	$7,680
		Less monthly fixed cost		$5,000
		Net operating profit		$2,680

A staff meeting was called to review the recommendation for replacing the possible loss of the wheel hub business. As Jim was illustrating the minor change in net operating profit, he explained that the $120 was attributable to the $.50 difference in the contribution of the wheel hub and gearbox.

$17.50 (Table 4.13) minus $17.00 (Table 7.4) = $.50 x 240 each = $120

They were all pleased to be able to tell Mr. Porter that the potential loss of the wheel hub business would result in a small decrease in profit of only $120 per month.

Optimization Techniques Do Not Mix Well with Traditional Thinking

Mr. Porter had been observing quietly as Jim and Reuben presented their case, but at this point he could no longer keep silent: "You have come a long way since relying on the standard cost system. I was impressed that when you evaluated the three new available parts you didn't even consider allocated fixed cost and/or gross profit calculations. Instead, you chose the part with the highest contribution without even considering its total standard cost. That's all well and fine, but what about what we've learned about optimization techniques? Will the part with the highest individual contribution automatically provide the highest total plant contribution and subsequent profit? If that were true, then why aren't we making brake calipers with a contribution of $19.00 instead of wheel hubs with a contribution of $17.50?"

Mr. Porter then instructed them to evaluate the three proposed parts using the OpTek Algorithm. The meeting was adjourned, and Jim and Reuben began to re-evaluate their proposal.

They formulated the objective and included the five existing parts plus all three new parts, i.e., gearbox, counterweight, and tie rod. Individual part contributions for these three new parts were calculated in Table 7.4.

Maximize $15.00(valve body) + $22.50(axle housing) + $10.00(differential case) + $17.50(wheel hub) + $19.00(brake caliper) + $17.00(gearbox) + $15.50(counterweight) + $14.00(tie rod)

(Subject to product routings per Tables 2.4 and 7.3 and departmental capacities per Table 2.4.)

The additional modification is to limit the number of wheel hubs to zero.

Wheel hubs = 0

Table 7.7 Product Mix and Contribution When Evaluating All Three of the New Parts With the OpTek Algorithm

Objective: **Maximize Contribution**					
Product	Qty.	Department	Hrs. Required	Slack	Opportunity
Valve bodies	129	Core	200	0	$4.12
Axle housings	87	Assembly	200	0	.88
Differential cases	0	Molding	200	0	21.09
Wheel hubs	0	Cleaning	200	0	10.48
Brake calipers	0	Grinding	200	0	3.78
Gearboxes	65				
Counterweights	20				
Tie rods	198				
Totals	500		1,000	0	
Maximum contribution possible $8,080					

One would have thought that by now Jim or Reuben couldn't be surprised by the results of optimization technology, but the results of this scenario caught them off guard. They noted several interesting facts:

1. Contribution had indeed increased by $400, from $7,680 in Table 7.6 to $8,080 in Table 7.7.
2. All three new parts, each with a contribution less than the wheel hub, appeared in the contribution maximizing product mix.
3. The part with the lowest contribution of the three new parts, i.e., the tie rod, reflects a proposed quantity greater than any of the other parts.
4. They noted that total quantity was now 500. The reason for this was that the 198 tie rods required only 99 molds. Its routing had revealed that two tie rods could be made in one mold.
5. They found it interesting that this proposed mix produced zero system slack, however, they knew not to equate this with profitability.

Optimization Techniques Should Prompt the Rethinking of Opportunities That Were Previously Rejected with Traditional Wisdom

When Mr. Porter reviewed the revised results, he too was a little surprised. The results caused him to wonder about the wisdom in maintaining their existing contracts to supply 160 axle housings and 240 wheel hubs: "Perhaps the dynamics of the business should make us rethink our degree of participation in this present market. Considering the new opportunity with gearboxes, counterweights, and tie rods, maybe we should shift into the market that includes these items."

"Reuben, optimization technology has shown us that we could actually improve our profitability if we were to lose the wheel hub business. I wonder, however, if it would be feasible to consider the new parts even if we did not lose the wheel hub business. In other words, should we be assertive in letting our wheel hub and axle housing contracts expire? Please review this idea and advise me which market focus will provide the most profit."

So Reuben and Jim went back to work. At first they didn't realize that all they had to do was run the algorithm without confining the quantity of wheel hubs to zero:

Maximize $15.00(valve body) + $22.50(axle housing) + $10.00(differential case) +
$17.50(wheel hub) + $19.00(brake caliper) + $17.00(gearbox) +
$15.50(counterweight) + $14.00(tie rod)

(Subject to product routings per Tables 2.4 and 7.3 and departmental capacities per Table 2.4.)

Table 7.8 Product Mix and Contribution When Considering all Eight Parts, i.e., the Original Five Plus the New Three

Objective: **Maximize Contribution**					
Product	**Qty.**	**Department**	**Hrs. Required**	**Slack**	**Opportunity**
Valve bodies	0	Core	188.72	11.28	0
Axle housings	51	Assembly	166.16	34.84	0
Differential cases	0	Molding	200.00	0	$31.64
Wheel hubs	205	Cleaning	200.00	0	7.56
Brake calipers	0	Grinding	200.00	0	4.61
Gearboxes	0				
Counterweights	0				
Tie rods	288				
Totals	**544**		**954.88**	**46.12**	
Maximum contribution possible $8,767					

The staff reconvened, and Jim and Reuben presented their findings.

1. OpTek's 400 mold capacity could now be used to produce 544 total parts due to the tie rod being molded two per mold.
2. Plant contribution would continue to improve if this mix were adopted.

Mr. Porter listened with great interest and made several of his own observations:

1. "We can take on new work that has a lower part contribution than the present work and still increase total plant profitability. I can't believe that we survived when we were tied to that old standard cost system."
2. "We must not get complacent when it comes to evaluating new work. It might on the surface appear to be undesirable but it really cannot be evaluated properly without a tool such as the OpTek Algorithm."

Jim then calculated their projected ROI, reflecting Table 7.8.

Contribution $8,767 × 12	= $105,204
Fixed cost $5,000 × 12	= $ 60,000
Net profit from operations	= $ 45,204

$$\text{ROI:} \quad \frac{\text{Change in assets}}{\text{Beginning assets}} = \frac{\text{Profit}}{\text{Beginning assets}} = \frac{\$45,204}{\$400,000} = 11.3\%$$

Summary—Key Points

We learned from this chapter that:

- Once again, if standard cost information is used to determine the financial impact of lost business or to make the choice as to replacement business, both aspects of the decision will be suboptimal.
- If any part of the decision process is diluted with traditional wisdom, the entire decision will be tainted and suboptimal.

This chapter showed how optimization technology does not mix well with traditional thinking. The following should be re-evaluated using optimization technology:

- Previous proposals that were rejected with traditional wisdom.
- Proposals already incorporated using traditional wisdom to ensure that the plant is operating at its potential profit level.

CHAPTER 8

Should We Be a Subcontractor?

If a plant has idle capacity in any of its nonconstrained departments or work centers, one of the initial reactions is to utilize such capacity. Of course, if a plant uses that capacity to produce existing work in advance, or at a rate that exceeds the output of its constraint, the result is excess work-in-process inventory.

The better alternative would be to consider bringing other work into the plant that does not require a constrained work center.

Such is the case with OpTek. It is considering bringing subcontracted work into its plant to utilize its work centers that contain idle capacity, i.e., slack when producing its present optimum product mix.

Optimization techniques will be used to evaluate the subcontracting opportunity. The subcontracting issue is not nearly as obvious as it might initially appear.

Chapter Contents

- Measuring the financial impact of a new idea
- Management myopia can be a major constraint
- The basic foundation remains the same: routings, capacities, and contributions
- Understanding the unexpected
- Reaping the consequence of limiting the power of optimization techniques

Measuring the Financial Impact of a New Idea

Jim and Reuben were visiting over a cup of coffee about the varied options available to OpTek to increase its monthly net operating profit. They recalled that they could get a 15.6 percent projected ROI by increased outsourcing activities and an 11.3 percent ROI by bringing new work into the plant. Jim asked Reuben if it were feasible or even possible to improve their financial performance by being a subcontractor, i.e., bringing part of a customer's manufacturing process into their facility. Reuben didn't have a ready answer, so they decided to invite Stephanie into their conversation.

Stephanie arrived shortly, and they asked her about the feasibility of being a subcontractor. She told them: "Because of the nature of our manufacturing process it would be feasible to do subcontract work but there are peculiarities involved. For example, the core and assembly operations should be done together. Also the cleaning and grinding operations should be done together. It is not feasible to subcontract the molding operation. Therefore, a primary producer could perform core, assembly, and molding and subcontract out the cleaning and grinding operations. Or the same producer might subcontract out the core and assembly operations and perform the molding, cleaning, and grinding operations.

"Let's go to the conference room and project the slide that reflects our present plant loading with our contribution maximizing product mix and see if there are any opportunities for subcontracting."

The benchmark product mix is reproduced as Table 8.1.

Table 8.1 OpTek's Benchmark Product Mix for Contribution Maximization

Product	Qty.	Department	Hrs. Required	Slack	Opportunity
Valve bodies	0	Core	200	0	$10.00
Axle housings	160	Assembly	80	120	0
Differential cases	0	Molding	200	0	$29.00
Wheel hubs	240	Cleaning	136	64	0
Brake calipers	0	Grinding	96	104	0
Totals	400		712	288	
Maximum contribution possible $7,800					

Jim said, "Let me get this straight. We can do core and assembly together, while the primary producer would perform molding, cleaning, and grinding. Or the primary producer could perform core, assembly, and molding and we would do cleaning and grinding together."

"That's right," confirmed Stephanie.

Management Myopia Can Be a Major Constraint

"If that is the case," said Jim, "we presently have no capacity to do the core and assembly operations together because we have an existing constraint in the core department. The 120 hours slack in the assembly department is therefore meaningless. And if we consider doing the cleaning and grinding together, we have in essence only 64 available hours because we need to consider the department with the least available time of the two, which is cleaning. The hours in excess of 64 in the grinding area have no value according to the process limitations."

Jim chuckled sarcastically as he left the meeting and commented, "Let's see what you two can do with 64 hours of spare capacity per month."

His sarcasm didn't deter Reuben or Stephanie because they remembered how wrong Jim had been relative to the outsourcing opportunities.

Reuben called the buyer at Crow-Bar and asked him if he would entertain a subcontracting proposal covering partial processing for the three parts that Crow-Bar had considered purchasing outright—gearboxes, counterweights, and tie rods. Crow-Bar indicated that it would be open to any proposal if that would be profitable for the company.

The Basic Foundation Remains the Same: Routings, Capacities, and Contributions

The first thing that Reuben and Stephanie did was to review the proposed routings for the three jobs in question. They had developed this information when they had considered producing the three parts in total.

Table 8.2 Projected Routings for the Three Jobs Being Considered for Partial
Process subcontracting

Department	Gearbox	Counterweight	Tie Rod
Core	.3	0	.3
Assembly	.2	0	.4
Molding	.5	.5	.25
Cleaning	.3	.4	.5
Grinding	.5	.2	.5

Next, Reuben determined the proposed prices to perform the core and assembly operations on these parts, and then he and Stephanie asked Jim to provide the projected variable costs to perform these two operations.

Table 8.3 Proposed Contributions for Performing the Core and Assembly Operations on the Gearbox, Counterweight, and Tie Rod for Crow-Bar

Contribution	Gearbox	Counterweight*	Tie Rod
Core	.3	0	.3
Assembly	.2	0	.4
Proposed price	$17.50	NA	$17.50
Estimated variable cost	$10.00	NA	$ 9.50
Proposed contribution	$ 7.50	NA	$ 8.00

The counterweight did not require a core because of its nomenclature.

With the above information, the required changes could be made to the routing matrix and the contribution maximizing objective formulated.

Table 8.4 Complete Routing Matrix Reflecting Routings of Three Proposed Jobs Processed in Core and Assembly

Department	Valve Body	Axle Housing	Diff. Case	Wheel Hub	Brake Caliper	Gear-box	Counter-weight	Tie Rod	Time Avail.
Core	.4	.8	.1	.3	.9	.3	0	.3	200
Assembly	.7	.2	.1	.2	.7	.2	0	.4	200
Molding	.5	.5	.5	.5	.5	0	0	0	200
Clean	.1	.7	.2	.1	.6	0	0	0	200
Grinding	.3	.3	.1	.2	.8	0	0	0	200

The objective becomes:

Maximize $15.00(valve body) + $22.50(axle housing) + $10.00(differential case) + $17.50(wheel hub) + $19.00(brake caliper) + $7.50(gearbox) + 0(counterweight) + $8.00(tie rod)

(Subject to the routing matrix and available time in Table 8.4.)

Table 8.5 Contribution Maximizing Product Mix When Performing Core and
Assembly Operations on Crow-Bar's Gearbox and Tie Rod

Objective: **Maximize Contribution**					
Product	Qty.	Department	Hrs. Required	Slack	Opportunity
Valve bodies	0	Core	200	0	$26.66
Axle housings	0	Assembly	187	13	0
Differential cases	0	Molding	200	0	$19.00
Wheel hubs	400	Cleaning	40	160	0
Brake calipers	0	Grinding	80	120	0
Gearboxes	0				
Counterweights	0				
Tie rods	267				
Totals	667		707	293	
Maximum contribution possible $9,136					

Jim arrived shortly and the three of them evaluated the results.

Understanding the Unexpected

Reuben continued: "Contribution would increase by 17.1 percent from our benchmark of $7,800 to the projected $9,136. Our total molding capacity would be used
to produce only wheel hubs. Our core and assembly capacity would process the
400 wheel hubs that we could mold and also process 267 tie rods. And look at the
plant utilization. It would slip to 70.7 percent while contribution increases by 17.1
percent. It appears that it would be a good idea to perform the core and assembly
processes on Crow-Bar's tie rods."

They all found the results to be very surprising.

"Let's evaluate the feasibility of running these same three parts through the
cleaning and grinding departments instead of core and assembly to see if more
contribution can be generated from the back end of the process."

From the projected routing matrix in Table 8.2, they estimated the proposed
prices to perform cleaning and grinding, and Jim estimated the variable cost to
perform these final two operations of the process.

Table 8.6 Proposed Contributions for Performing the Cleaning and Grinding Operations on the Gearbox, Counterweight, and Tie Rod for Crow-Bar

Contribution	Gearbox	Counterweight*	Tie Rod
Cleaning	.3	.4	.5
Grinding	.5	.2	.5
Proposed price	$10.00	$10.00	$10.00
Estimated variable cost	$ 4.00	$ 5.00	$ 3.00
Proposed contribution	$ 6.00	$ 5.00	$ 7.00

The routing matrix is amended to reflect this scenario of performing the cleaning and grinding operations on the gearboxes, counterweights, and tie rods.

Table 8.7 Routing Matrix Changes to Reflect Performing the Cleaning and Grinding Operations on Crow-Bar's Gearboxes, Counterweights, and Tie Rods

Department	Gearbox	Counterweight	Tie Rod	Time Available
Core	0	0	0	200 hrs.
Assembly	0	0	0	200 hrs.
Molding	0	0	0	200 hrs.
Cleaning	.3	.4	.5	200 hrs.
Grinding	.5	.2	.5	200 hrs.

The objective becomes:

Maximize $15.00(valve body) + $22.50(axle housing) + $10.00(differential case) + $17.50(wheel hub) + $19.00(brake caliper) + $6.00(gearbox) + $5.00(counterweight) + $7.00(tie rod)

(Subject to the product routings and departmental capacities per Tables 8.4 and 8.7.)

Table 8.8 Contribution Maximizing Product Mix When Performing Cleaning and Grinding Operations on Crow-Bar's Gearboxes, Counterweights, and Tie Rods

Objective: **Maximize Contribution**					
Product	Qty.	Department	Hrs. Required	Slack	Opportunity
Valve bodies	0	Core	120	80	0
Axle housings	0	Assembly	80	120	0
Differential cases	0	Molding	200	0	$30.57
Wheel hubs	400	Cleaning	200	0	$ 9.28
Brake calipers	0	Grinding	200	0	$ 6.42
Gearboxes	114				
Counterweights	314				
Tie rods	0				
Totals	828		800	200	
Maximum contribution possible $9,254					

Reuben was impressed: "The contribution is even more than when we considered doing the core and assembly operations on those parts. The molding machine would still produce all wheel hubs with this scenario. The cleaning and grinding departments would become constrained as they processed the 400 wheel hubs that we would mold plus 114 gearboxes and 314 counterweights for Crow-Bar. I had no idea this potential existed."

"What is really interesting is the fact that the individual contributions on these three parts for the cleaning and grinding operations are less than if we performed the core and assembly operations, and yet total plant contribution is more."

Table 8.9 Individual Part Contributions for Gearboxes, Counterweights, and Tie Rods for Core and Assembly or Cleaning and Grinding

Contribution	Gearbox	Counterweight	Tie Rod
Core and assembly	$7.50	0	$8.00
Cleaning and grinding	$6.00	$5.00	$7.00

In fact, both of the subcontracting opportunities produce more contribution than when we considered making the total parts for Crow-Bar. The contribution produced when we considered performing all operations was $8,767 per month per Table 7.8, and I thought that was great.

"We need to call the boss now and show him the two available subcontracting opportunities. He will be so pleased to see what we can do with 64 hours of capacity."

Mr. Porter came into the conference room and listened intently as Reuben and Stephanie illustrated the two subcontracting opportunities. They highlighted several issues:

1. Total plant contribution in both cases exceeded the contribution opportunity if OpTek performed all operations when they were considering bringing new work into the plant.
2. In both opportunities, the base mix for the molding machine would be 400 wheel hubs.
3. It appeared that the tie rod was a good prospect for performing the core and assembly operations, while the gearbox and counterweight were not.
4. Conversely the gearbox and counterweight were good prospects for performing the cleaning and grinding operations, while the tie rod was not.

Reuben wanted to act: "I'll contact Crow-Bar and advise them of our interest to perform cleaning and grinding on their gearboxes and counterweights. Our contribution with this scenario would be $9,254 versus $9,136 if we performed core and assembly on their tie rods."

Mr. Porter wasn't sure Reuben had thought it all through. Reuben confirmed: "The total plant contribution is in fact more if we process their gearboxes and counterweights in cleaning and grinding."

But Mr. Porter had two questions:

Question: How much slack would be in the plant and where would it be with the scenario of processing the tie rods in core and assembly?

Answer: There would be 160 hours slack in cleaning and 120 hours slack in the grinding department, per Table 8.5.

Question: How much and where would the slack be in the plant, if any, with the scenario of processing the gearboxes and counterweights in cleaning and grinding?

Answer: There would be 80 hours slack in core and 120 hours slack in assembly, per Table 8.8.

Reuben was a little sheepish as he acknowledged that perhaps they could combine scenarios, i.e., perform core and assembly operations on the tie rods while simultaneously performing the cleaning and grinding operations on the gearboxes and counterweights. Then they together developed the proposed routing matrix and objective to combine scenarios.

Table 8.10 Routings and Respective Contributions to Process Tie Rods in Core and Assembly and Gearboxes and Counterweights in Cleaning and Grinding

Contribution	Gearbox	Counterweight	Tie Rod
Core	.3	0	.3
Assembly	.2	0	.4
Cleaning	.3	.4	.5
Grinding	.5	.2	.5
Proposed price	$10.00	$10.00	$17.50
Estimated variable cost	$ 4.00	$ 5.00	$ 9.50
Proposed contribution	$ 6.00	$ 5.00	$ 8.00

The objective becomes:

Maximize $15.00(valve body) + $22.50(axle housing) + $10.00(differential case) + $17.50(wheel hub) + $19.00(brake caliper) + $6.00(gearbox) + $5.00(counterweight) + $8.00(tie rod)

(Subject to product routings and departmental capacities per Tables 8.4 and 8.10.)

Table 8.11 Maximum Contribution When Performing Core and Assembly Operations on Tie Rods and Cleaning and Grinding on Gearboxes and Counterweights

Objective: **Maximize Contribution**

Product	Qty.	Department	Hrs. Required	Slack	Opportunity
Valve bodies	0	Core	200	0	$26.66
Axle housing	0	Assembly	187	13	0
Differential cases	0	Molding	200	0	$14.57
Wheel hubs	400	Cleaning	200	0	$ 9.28
Brake calipers	0	Grinding	200	0	$ 6.42
Gearboxes	114				
Counterweights	314				
Tie rods	267				
Totals	1,095		987	13	
Maximum contribution possible $11,390					

Reuben noticed the synergistic effect of combining scenarios almost immediately.

Incremental contribution if processing tie rods in core and assembly ($9,136 from Table 8.5 less benchmark of $7,800)   = $1,336

Incremental contribution if processing gear-boxes and counterweights in cleaning and grinding ($9,254 from Table 8.8 less benchmark of $7,800)   = $1,454

Total incremental contribution when considering both alternatives in isolation   = $2,790

Incremental contribution when combining scenarios (tie rods in core and assembly and gearboxes and counterweights in cleaning and grinding ($11,390 from Table 8.11 less benchmark of $7,800)   = $3,590

Synergistic advantage   = $ 800

Mr. Porter asked Jim to display Table 8.11 in the variable income statement format and calculate the projected productivity of capital and ROI.

Table 8.12 Variable Costing Income Statement Reflecting Subcontracting Opportunities for Gearboxes, Counterweights, and Tie Rods

OpTek Corporation

Variable Costing Income Statement

Product	Qty.	Molds	Revenue	Variable Cost	Contribution
Wheel hubs	400	400	$14,000	$ 7,000	$ 7,000
Gearboxes	114	0	$ 1,140	$ 456	$ 684
Counterweights	314	0	$ 3,140	$ 1,570	$ 1,570
Tie rods	267	0	$ 4,673	$ 2,537	$ 2,136
Totals	**1,095**	**400**	**$22,953**	**$11,563**	**$11,390**
			Less facility fixed cost		$5,000
			Net operating profit		**$6,390**

$$\textbf{Capital Productivity: } \frac{\text{Ending assets}}{\text{Beginning assets}} = \frac{\text{Output}}{\text{Input}} = \frac{\$476,680^*}{\$400,000} = 1.192$$

* $6,390 Monthly profit $\times$ 12 = $76,680 Annual profit + Beginning assets
= $400,000 = Output, or ending assets

$$\textbf{ROI: } \frac{\text{Ending assets} - \text{Beginning assets}}{\text{Beginning assets}} = \frac{\text{Profit}}{\text{Beginning assets}} = \frac{\$76,680}{\$400,000} = 19.2\%$$

Needless to say, Mr. Porter was exceedingly pleased with the subcontracting opportunities. Total plant contribution had increased 46 percent from the benchmark of $7,800 to the projected $11,390. And it was all possible within their primary molding constraint of 400 molds!

By subcontracting work into its plant, OpTek's financial opportunity would exceed the financial opportunity provided by the alternatives of increased outsourcing activity and bring new work into the plant. Mr. Porter realized, however, that the relative desirability of these options could change with variations in the basic building blocks of routings, capacities, and contributions.

Reaping the Consequence of Limiting the Power of Optimization Techniques

Before they left the meeting Mr. Porter invited them all to his home the next day for a cookout. Jim had very little to say, while Reuben went crow hunting and Stephanie went to buy a skewer.

Summary—Key Points

This chapter explained that:

- What may appear on the surface to be a very limited opportunity for profit improvement may actually have tremendous profit potential.
- Confidence in optimization techniques does overcome management myopia.
- The basic foundation remains the same when evaluating a new idea, i.e., contributions, routings, and capacities.
- Traditional thinking would immediately eliminate the subcontracting opportunity in most plants (especially those similar to OpTek's specific example), because on the surface there is insufficient capacity in the plant to bring in any additional work.

SECTION V

Selective Growth and System Expansion Using Optimization Techniques

CHAPTER 9

Optimizing the Capital Budget with Better Measurement of the Financial Benefits from Proposed Equipment Additions

This chapter will introduce optimization techniques to the capital budgeting decision process.

One of the major challenges relative to capital equipment decisions centers on the identification of the projected financial benefits associated with a given proposal. Optimization techniques will provide the operating cash flow for a capital proposal much more accurately than traditional wisdom and much quicker.

Chapter Contents

- Making capital improvements in nonconstrained departments has limited value
- The capital budget must begin with constrained departments
- The utilization of proposed equipment should not be a major decision factor
- Automatic determination of proposed equipment's cash flow
- Optimization techniques in the area of capital budgeting produces results not possible with the best of intuition
- Tremendous synergy is possible when removing multiple constraints simultaneously

OpTek's staff has certainly learned a great deal about optimization technology in recent months. They have learned:

1. The inherent weaknesses of using standard cost systems.
2. That contribution maximization is the strategy that will maximize net operating profit.
3. How to measure the real impact of making manufacturing process improvements.
4. How to measure the real impact of the make-or-buy decision.
5. How to evaluate the relative desirability of new business.
6. How to measure the financial impact of being a subcontractor.

Now they are considering adding capacity to their plant, and they wish to use optimization technology to get the most from their capital budget.

Not only do they wish to optimize their capital budget, they want to avoid those areas where capital spending would have little or no effect on total system contribution and profitability. Attempting to justify capital projects in isolation will lead to suboptimization and unwise investment decisions. Their starting point will once again be their benchmark mix, reproduced here as Table 9.1.

Table 9.1 OpTek's Benchmark Product Mix for Contribution Maximization

Objective: **Maximize Contribution**					
Product	Qty.	Department	Hrs. Required	Slack	Opportunity
Valve bodies	0	Core	200	0	$10.00
Axle housings	160	Assembly	80	120	0
Differential cases	0	Molding	200	0	29.00
Wheel hubs	240	Cleaning	136	64	0
Brake calipers	0	Grinding	96	104	0
Totals	400		712	288	
Maximum contribution possible $7,800					

As the staff members studied Table 9.1, they could see that there were two constrained departments in their plant—core and molding. Up to this point, they had been working within the confines of these constraints. But now they were considering increasing the capacity of these constrained departments. The challenge would be how to measure the financial benefit from such actions.

Making Capital Improvements in Nonconstrained Departments Has Limited Value

However, before they began to simulate the results from adding capacity to constrained departments, Jim wanted to prove a point about the futility of making improvements, either in the form of process improvements or capacity additions, to nonconstrained departments: "There are three departments in the plant that are not constrained with our optimum product mix in Table 9.1. They are assembly, cleaning, and grinding. Now, even though both axle housings and wheel hubs, the two products in our contribution maximizing product mix, are routed through these nonconstrained departments, any improvement in process times in these three departments would have *no* effect on plant contribution."

Jim directed their attention to the original routing matrix that is reproduced here as Table 9.2.

Table 9.2 Routing Matrix for OpTek Corporation

	Product					
Department	Valve Body	Axle Housing	Differential Case	Wheel Hub	Brake Caliper	**Time Available**
Core	.4	.8	.1	.3	.9	200 hrs.
Assembly	.7	.2	.1	.2	.7	200 hrs.
Molding	.5	.5	.5	.5	.5	200 hrs.
Cleaning	.1	.7	.2	.1	.6	200 hrs.
Grinding	.3	.3	.1	.2	.8	200 hrs.

He said: "If Ben could come up with some miraculous engineering improvements that would reduce the process times by 50 percent on all five parts in all three of the nonconstrained departments, the only result would be more slack in those departments."

They proceeded to revise the routing matrix to be able to simulate this scenario.

Table 9.3 Routing Matrix Adjusted to Reflect All Processing Times in All Three Nonconstrained Departments Reduced by 50 Percent

| | Product | | | | | |
Department	Valve Body	Axle Housing	Differential Case	Wheel Hub	Brake Caliper	Time Available
Core	.4	.8	.1	.3	.9	200 hrs.
Assembly	.35	.1	.05	.1	.35	200 hrs.
Molding	.5	.5	.5	.5	.5	200 hrs.
Cleaning	.05	.35	.1	.05	.3	200 hrs.
Grinding	.15	.15	.05	.1	.4	200 hrs.

Using contribution maximization as the objective, they ran the algorithm incorporating the routing alterations in Table 9.3 above with the following results:

Table 9.4 The Results of Process Time Changes in Nonconstrained Departments

Objective: **Maximize Contribution**

Product	Qty.	Department	Hrs. Required	Slack	Opportunity
Valve bodies	0	Core	200	0	$10.00
Axle housings	160	Assembly	48	152	0
Differential cases	0	Molding	200	0	29.00
Wheel hubs	240	Cleaning	68	132	0
Brake calipers	0	Grinding	48	152	0
Totals	400		564	436	
Maximum contribution possible $7,800					

The results were straightforward. Proposed process changes that involve time reductions in nonconstrained departments have no effect on total plant contribution. The most striking effect was that slack, or idle time, increased from 288 hours to 436 hours, or 51 percent.

It was pointed out that the only effect of such process improvements is the ability to produce excess work-in-process inventory quicker. Not the way to go. Jim did point out, however, that if the proposed process changes illustrated above resulted in variable cost reductions, the result would have been an increase in contribution.

The Capital Budget Must Begin with Constrained Departments

Now the attention was focused on the constrained departments. Jim refreshed their memories as to the meaning of the "opportunity" column on the far right of Table 9.1: "If we could add one hour of capacity to the core department, total plant contribution would increase $10.00 per month. If we could add one hour of capacity to molding, then total plant contribution would increase $29.00 per month."

Stephanie wondered what good it would do to add capacity to just one department if two of them are constrained? Obviously, for the moment she had lost the concept of optimization techniques.

They agreed that they needed to experiment and do some simulations before drafting the capital budget. They knew for sure, however, that the starting point would be their existing constrained departments, so they began with the core department. Their initial objective was to learn how to measure the financial benefits provided by the proposed expansion. They would later justify the capital cost of the expansion.

They reviewed the product routings relative to the core department found originally in Table 2.4 (p. 16) and partially reproduced here as Table 9.5.

Table 9.5 Existing Product Routing and Capacity of the Core Department

Department	Product					Time Available
	Valve Body	Axle Housing	Differential Case	Wheel Hub	Brake Caliper	
Core	.4	.8	.1	.3	.9	200 hrs.

The only change that was required to be made to the data set was to amend the time available to the core department.

Table 9.6 Existing Product Routing and Projected Capacity of the Core Department

Department	Product					Time Available
	Valve Body	Axle Housing	Differential Case	Wheel Hub	Brake Caliper	
Core	.4	.8	.1	.3	.9	400 hrs.

With this one simple modification, Jim could activate the OpTek Algorithm with the common objective of contribution maximization:

Maximize $15.00(valve body) + $22.50(axle housing) + $10.00(differential case) +
$17.50(wheel hub) + $19.00(brake caliper)

(Subject to product routings and departmental capacities per Tables 2.4 [p. 16] and 9.6.)

Table 9.7 Product Mix and Contribution Resulting from Increasing Core Department Capacity to 400 Hours

Objective: **Maximize Contribution**					
Product	**Qty.**	**Department**	**Hrs. Required**	**Slack**	**Opportunity**
Valve bodies	0	**Core**	**253.34**	**146.66**	0
Axle housings	267	Assembly	80.00	120.00	0
Differential cases	0	Molding	200.00	0	$33.33
Wheel hubs	133	Cleaning	200.00	0	8.33
Brake calipers	0	Grinding	106.67	93.33	0
Totals	**400**		**840.01**	**359.99**	
Maximum contribution possible $8,335					

This table really initiated some lively discussion among the staff. They noted several items of interest:

1. Contribution did in fact increase by $535, from $7,800 to $8,335.
2. The same two products were involved, i.e., axle housings and wheel hubs, but in a substantially different ratio. The additional core capacity was better utilized by more axle housings, which had a higher contribution than the wheel hubs. The total number of parts remained 400 because of the fact that molding was still constrained.

   The opportunity for molding increased from $29.00 to $33.00 as molding time became more valuable in light of increased core capacity.
3. As core capacity increased, the core department was no longer constrained; however, a new constraint surfaced—cleaning.

The Utilization of Proposed Equipment Should Not Be a Major Decision Factor

Stephanie was really concerned about the projected utilization in the core department with the additional equipment. She noted that the utilization of the new core machine was only 26.7 percent.

The projected core capacity would be 400 hours. Inasmuch as there is now 146.66 hours of slack in the core department, the additional core capacity of 200 hours was only utilized by 200 − 146.66 = 53.34 hours.

$$\frac{53.34 \text{ used hours}}{200 \text{ new available hours}} = 26.7\% \text{ Utilization}$$

Mr. Porter told them that the utilization factor must be *subsidiary* to the more important aspect of the amount of increased plant contribution provided by the proposed addition of core capacity.

Automatic Determination of Proposed Equipment's Cash Flow

He further commented: "Perhaps the most difficult aspect of capital project justification is the determination of the cash flow to be expected for a capital proposal. People like Stephanie, Reuben, and Ben try to estimate revenue and expenses in an attempt to quantify the net cash flow expected.

"At best, however, they are limited to isolated thinking. Without the OpTek Algorithm they cannot visualize the simultaneous interactions of product routings and departmental capacities. *Optimization technology, however, provides the relevant cash flow automatically.* It is really very simple. The incremental contribution of $535 provided by the additional core capacity *is* the relevant *cash flow* for this proposal."

Now it was time to consider the other constraint in the system—molding. The molding operation had an opportunity of $29.00 per hour.

Once again the only change in the data set was to increase the available hours in the molding department from 200 to 400 per the following:

Table 9.8 Existing Product Routing and Projected Capacity of the Molding Department

	Product					
Department	Valve Body	Axle Housing	Differential Case	Wheel Hub	Brake Caliper	**Time Available**
Molding	.5	.5	.5	.5	.5	**400 hours**

With this change in the data set the OpTek Algorithm could be activated with contribution maximization as the objective:

Maximize $15.00(valve body) + $22.50(axle housing) + $10.00(differential case) + $17.50(wheel hub) + $19.00(brake caliper)

(Subject to product routings per Table 2.4 and departmental capacity per Table 9.8.)

Table 9.9 Product Mix and Contribution Resulting from Adding 200 Hours to Molding Department

Objective: **Maximize Contribution**					
Product	**Qty.**	**Department**	**Hrs. Required**	**Slack**	**Opportunity**
Valve bodies	0	Core	200	0	$37.50
Axle housings	0	Assembly	140	60	0
Differential cases	200	**Molding**	**400**	0	12.50
Wheel hubs	600	Cleaning	100	100	0
Brake calipers	0	Grinding	140	60	0
Totals	**800**		980	220	
Maximum contribution possible $12,500					

Optimzation Techniques in the Area of Capital Budgeting Produces Results Not Possible with the Best of Intuition

The analysis of Table 9.9 revealed several significant facts. They all agreed that intuition would never have predicted this outcome.

1. The increase in contribution was substantially more when adding 200 hours to the molding department than by adding 200 hours to the core department:

	Core Department	*Molding Department*
Contribution after	$8,335 (Table 9.7)	$12,500 (Table 9.9)
Contribution before	7,800 (Table 9.1)	7,800 (Table 9.1)
Incremental contribution	**$ 535**	**$ 4,700**

2. The addition of 200 hours to the molding department capacity allowed for 800 total molds/parts to be produced.

Before
$$\frac{200 \text{ hrs.}}{.5 \text{ hrs. each}} = 400$$

After
$$\frac{400 \text{ hrs.}}{.5 \text{ hrs. each}} = 800$$

3. Clearly, one-fourth of the new mix, i.e., 200 parts, would be differential cases. This caused all of them to scratch their heads because the individual contribution of the differential case was by far the lowest of the five available products for the algorithm to choose.

Product	Individual Contribution	Ranking by Contribution
Valve body	$15.00	4
Axle housing	22.50	1
Differential Case	**10.00**	**5**
Wheel hub	17.50	3
Brake caliper	19.00	2

4. Three-fourths of the mix, i.e., 600 parts were wheel hubs, which were also far from having the highest contribution.

5. The two parts with the highest individual contribution, i.e., axle housing and brake caliper, were rejected, while the part with the lowest individual contribution, differential case, was selected.

   Once again the algorithm displayed its ability to do what was best for the entire plant's financial well-being.

6. As explained previously, the relevant cash flow associated with the proposal to expand molding capacity was $4,700 per month:

   $12,500 per Table 9.9 – $7,800 per Table 9.1 = $4,700

If OpTek had sufficient capital would it be financially feasible to add capacity to core and molding departments simultaneously?

Incremental contribution by adding 200 hours capacity to core department	$ 535
Incremental contribution by adding 200 hours capacity to molding department	$ 4,700
Total Incremental cash flow by adding capacity to both	**$5,235**

Tremendous Synergy Is Possible When Removing Multiple Constraints Simultaneously

Mr. Porter asked Jim if there would be any synergy by adding capacity to both departments simultaneously, similar to the benefits when making multiple process improvements simultaneously. Jim could not answer without checking with the OpTek Algorithm. The data set required two small modifications, per Table 9.10.

Table 9.10 Routing Matrix and Departmental Capacities When Adding Capacity to Both Core and Molding Departments

	Product					
Department	Valve Body	Axle Housing	Differential Case	Wheel Hub	Brake Caliper	**Time Available**
Core	.4	.8	.1	.3	.9	**400 hrs.**
Assembly	.7	.2	.1	.2	.7	200 hrs.
Molding	.5	.5	.5	.5	.5	**400 hrs.**
Cleaning	.1	.7	.2	.1	.6	200 hrs.
Grinding	3	.3	.1	.2	.8	200 hrs.

Maximize $15.00(valve body) + $22.50(axle housing) + $10.00(differential case) + $17.50(wheel hub) + $19.00(brake caliper)

(Subject to product routings and departmental capacities per Table 9.10.)

Table 9.11 Product Mix and Contribution Resulting From Adding 200 Hours Capacity to Both Core and Molding Simultaneously

Objective: **Maximize Contribution**					
Product	**Qty.**	**Department**	**Hrs. Required**	**Slack**	**Opportunity**
Valve bodies	0	**Core**	340	60	0
Axle housings	200	Assembly	160	40	0
Differential cases	0	**Molding**	400	0	$33.33
Wheel hubs	600	Cleaning	200	0	8.33
Brake calipers	0	Grinding	180	20	0
Totals	800		1,280	120	
Maximum contribution possible $15,000					

Mr. Porter's question about synergy was certainly answered. The increase in contribution when adding capacity to both core and molding simultaneously was $7,200, which was substantially more than the $5,235 when considering these projects in isolation. Jim pointed out that the $15,000 proposed contribution was a full 92.3 percent more than with the benchmark mix of $7,800 in Table 9.1: "This is the way to do capital planning."

Mr. Porter replied: "We have learned once again that *product and departmental decisions made in isolation may not and most likely will not maximize profitability.* We have also learned the futility of improving manufacturing process times in nonconstrained departments. The results obtained by relieving departmental constraints could not have been determined without evaluating the numerous interactions generated as products compete for scarce work center capacity. *Optimization technology is a requisite for profit maximization, or anything even close to it.*"

OpTek's staff was now ready to equate the cash flows determined in this session with the capital investment required for the capacity additions in the constrained departments as they developed their capital budget.

Summary—Key Points

This chapter introduced several significant issues associated with the capital budgeting decision process:

- The proposed cash flow for a capital proposal developed with traditional methods will always be understated as compared to using optimization technology.
- Proposed operating improvements in nonconstrained work centers have limited or no value.
- The projected utilization of the proposed equipment should not be a major issue; rather, the total increase in plant contribution is the major issue.
- The projected cash flow attributed to a given proposal is calculated automatically by comparing total plant contribution before the proposal with the total plant contribution including the proposal.
- Capital budgeting following optimization techniques produces results highly superior to those following the best intuition.
- There is significant financial synergy achieved with the removal of multiple constraints simultaneously.

CHAPTER 10

Rethinking Traditional Capital Project Ranking Techniques

This chapter will present a new method of justifying and subsequently ranking competing capital proposals.

There are basically two major aspects of the capital budgeting decision: first, determining the proposed financial benefit of the proposed equipment and, second, comparing the proposed benefit with the cost to acquire that benefit.

Chapter Contents

- Illustrating the traditional method of ranking capital projects
- Optimization techniques consider the investment opportunity relative to its effect on total plant ROI
- Project rankings determined with traditional methods are substantially different than when determined with optimization techniques
- Plotting OpTek's financial progress as it learns to use optimization techniques

OpTek's staff had recently focused on measuring the financial benefits, or incremental cash flow, generated by proposed capital additions. Now they will direct their attention to the comparison of the anticipated cash flows from relieving their constraints with the investment required to relieve them. After this evaluation, OpTek will develop a ranking of its investment choices and develop its capital budget.

After completing the normal bid process, OpTek's staff determined the capital requirements to add capacity to the core and molding departments per Table 10.1.

Table 10.1 Capital Required to Add Capacity to the Core and Molding Departments

Department	Capital Required for New Equipment
Core	$ 15,000
Molding	$200,000
Core and molding simultaneously	$215,000

For their initial evaluation, OpTek ranked these projects based on their simple nondiscounted rate of return. They had previously determined the incremental cash flow (contribution) provided by capacity additions to the core and molding department.

Table 10.2 Summary of Cash Flows Generated from Capacity Additions

Department	Incremental Cash Flow	Source
Core	$ 535	Table 9.7 – Table 9.1
Molding	$4,700	Table 9.9 – Table 9.1
Both Core and Molding	$7,200	Table 9.11

Illustrating the Traditional Method of Ranking Capital Projects

Traditionally, the next step is to determine the *internal rate of return (IRR)* for each of the alternatives listed in Table 10.1. Remember, however, that OpTek is going to develop simple nondiscounted rates of return for their initial comparison. Therefore, the nondiscounted rate of return to add capacity to the core department is:

$$\frac{\text{Annual cash flow}}{\text{Investment required (Table 10.1)}} = \frac{\$535 \times 12}{\$15,000} = \frac{\$ 6,420}{\$15,000} = 42.8\%$$

Similarly, the nondiscounted rate of return to add capacity to the molding department is:

$$\frac{\text{Annual cash flow}}{\text{Investment required}} = \frac{\$4,700 \times 12}{\$200,000} = \frac{\$56,400}{\$200,000} = 28.2\%$$
(Table 10.1)

Finally, the nondiscounted rate of return to add capacity to the core and molding departments simultaneously is:

$$\frac{\text{Annual cash flow}}{\text{Investment required}} = \frac{\$7,200 \times 12}{\$215,000} = \frac{\$86,400}{\$215,000} = 40.2\%$$
(Table 10.1)

Now, if OpTek were to rank these investment opportunities in the traditional fashion, the ranking would appear as shown below.

Table 10.3 Summary of Traditional Rankings for Capacity Additions

Project Description	Nondiscounted ROI	Traditional Ranking
Add capacity to core	42.8%	1
Add capacity to molding	28.2%	3
Add capacity to both	40.2%	2

Optimization Techniques Consider the Investment Opportunity Relative to Its Effect on Total Plant ROI

OpTek's staff, however, had been introduced to the concept of optimization. They realized that they could not optimize their capital budget if they considered each project in isolation. *Each proposed capital addition must be evaluated in relation to the plant's total financial system.* So they began by re-evaluating the core department proposal, and the results were substantially different.

Table 10.4 OpTek's Total System ROI After Core Department Capacity Addition

Annual contribution after capacity addition to core department ($8,335 [Table 9.7] x 12 = $100,020)			= $100,020
Less annual fixed cost ($5,000 x 12)			$ 60,000
OpTek's annual net operating profit			$ 40,020
Total system ROI = $\dfrac{\text{Annual profits}}{\text{Total assets}}$	=	$\dfrac{\$ 40,020}{\$415,000^*}$	= 9.64%

*Total beginning assets + Cost of core capacity addition, per Table 10.1.

Then they re-evaluated the real financial benefit of adding capacity to the molding department.

Table 10.5 OpTek's Total System ROI After Molding Department Capacity Addition

Annual contribution after capacity addition to modling department ($12,500 [Table 9.9] x 12 = $150,000)			= $150,000
Less annual fixed cost ($5,000 x 12)			$ 60,000
OpTek's annual net operating profit			$ 90,000
Total system ROI = $\dfrac{\text{Annual profits}}{\text{Total assets}}$	=	$\dfrac{\$90,0000}{\$600,000^*}$	= 15.0%

Total beginning assets + Cost of molding capacity addition, per Table 10.1.

Lastly, they re-evaluated the proposal to add capacity to both core and molding departments simultaneously.

Table 10.6 OpTek's Total System ROI After Both Core and Molding Department Capacity Additions

Annual contribution after capacity addition to core and molding department ($15,000 [Table 9.11] x 12 = $180,000)			= $180,000
Less annual fixed cost ($5,000 x 12)			$ 60,000
OpTek's annual net operating profit			$120,000
Total system ROI = $\dfrac{\text{Annual profits}}{\text{Total assets}}$	=	$\dfrac{\$120,0000}{\$615,000^*}$	= 19.5%

Total beginning assets + Cost of core and mold capacity addition, per Table 10.1.

Jim was fully aware that depreciation for the proposed equipment was not included in the annual fixed cost calculation. He explained that he was at this point more interested in the ability to rank the proposals according to their impact on incremental contribution. He added, however, that the measurement could be done with or without depreciation.

Project Rankings Determined with Traditional Methods Are Substantially Different Than When Determined with Optimization Techniques

Now Jim was ready to develop a new ranking based on total system improvement.

Table 10.7 Project Ranking According to Impact on OpTek's Total Financial System

Project Description	Nondiscounted Isolated ROI	Traditional Ranking	Total System ROI	Integrative Ranking
Add capacity to core	42.8%	1	9.6%	3
Add capacity to molding	28.2%	3	15.0%	2
Add capacity to core and molding simultaneously	40.2%	2	19.5%	1

As Jim was showing his finding to the rest of the staff, he highlighted several things relative to this new method of project ranking:

1. The greatest difference was to be found in the ranking for adding capacity to the core department. This project appeared to be the most desirable when being ranked in the traditional manner, but it was in fact the least desirable when ranked relative to total system ROI.
2. It was very evident that all of the rankings changed when ranking the projects according to their total system impact versus ranking them in isolation.

Plotting OpTek's Financial Progress As It Learns to Use Contemporary Optimization Technology

Before Jim finished his part of the presentation, he summarized OpTek's progress since they had discovered the advantages of optimization technology. He listed the major milestones on their journey.

Table 10.8 Major Milestones in OpTek's Progress

Performance Measure	Starting Point (Table 2.13)	Initial Optimum Product Mix (Table 4.14)	After the Make-or-Buy Decision (Table 6.6)	After Capacity Additions (Table 9.11)
Monthly contribution	$6,720	$7,800	$10,200	$15,000
Plant ROI	5.2%	8.4%	15.6%	19.5%
Break-even percent molding capacity	74.5%	64.0%	49.0%	33.0%

Mr. Porter expressed his satisfaction with the progress they had made. He pointed out the fact that contribution was 223 percent higher while ROI had increased by 375 percent: "With all of your help, we have identified and done our best to cease committing the seven deadly sins of manufacturing. Likewise, I'm truly delighted with the results produced from optimization technology. We will really have a chance to use the knowledge gained over the last several months. It's about time to begin work on next year's aggregate plan, and we will incorporate optimization technology in its construction."

Summary—Key Points

In this chapter we learned:

- The optimization techniques associated with capital proposal ranking require that the investment/benefit results are expressed in terms of a plant's total financial position (in particular, the total plant ROI).
- A capital proposal evaluated in the traditional manner (while perhaps providing a relatively higher individual internal rate of return) may not provide the same impact to the total financial system as a proposal with a relatively lower individual internal rate of return.
- Using the concepts of optimization technology provides a different ranking of competing capital proposals.

SECTION VI

Illustrating the Aggregate Planning Process

CHAPTER 11

Developing the Aggregate Plan Using Optimization Techniques

The aggregate planning process in the OpTek continuing example will be substantially different than in previous years. For example, such terms as overhead absorption, departmental utilization, and gross profit will not be part of the aggregate planning process.

The current chapter will introduce optimization techniques into the aggregate planning process by considering the effect of cost and price changes.

Chapter Contents

- The aggregate planning process is much easier using optimization techniques
- Forecasting relies on internal manufacturing strengths as well as external market factors
- Measuring the impact of price increases
- Measuring the impact of variable cost increases
- Variable cost increases are measured relative to their impact on product contributions

Reuben, Stephanie, and Jim had received an email from their boss several weeks earlier advising them that there would be a planning session for next year's forecast and manufacturing budget on October 20. Well, this was the day, and they found themselves in the conference room for a planning session that they knew would be unlike any such session in the past.

The Aggregate Planning Process Is Much Easier Using Optimization Techniques

Conspicuously missing in this year's planning and budgeting session would be such items as "normal capacity," i.e., the level of activity that should absorb all the fixed overhead and calculation of overhead rates, and other factors. Plant utilization and overhead transfers would also not be issues in this planning session. Mr. Porter said: "Some of the production cost increases are beyond our control, however, we have certainly learned how to work with such factors and integrate them into our planning process. While most of the cost increases will be offset with increased selling prices, they could trigger changes in our business. We need to watch them very closely. This means we must be flexible and be able to respond to the dynamics of the markets we serve.

"As stated in my email, I would like each of you to address the planning items in your respective areas and, in fact, show the rest of us what the financial impact of each of these items will be."

Forecasting Relies on Internal Manufacturing Strengths As Well As External Market Factors

He continued: "We have not come into this meeting with a predetermined specific product forecast. We will develop that level of forecast detail after we define our optimum product mix based on various economic factors and build on some of the operational improvements we have done in our plant during the past year. The forecast must reflect the well-being of our most important constituency, i.e., OpTek's owners. Therefore, the starting point will be our present optimum product mix and its accompanying contribution."

This mix is reproduced here as Table 11.1.

Table 11.1 Present Contribution Maximizing Product Mix

Product	Qty.	Department	Hrs. Required	Slack	Opportunity
Valve bodies	0	Core	200	0	$10.00
Axle housings	160	Assembly	80	120	0
Differential cases	0	Molding	200	0	29.00
Wheel hubs	240	Cleaning	136	64	0
Brake calipers	0	Grinding	96	104	0
Totals	400		712	288	
Maximum contribution possible $7,800					

Measuring the Impact of Price Increases

Reuben began to give an overview of the price increases that the market will support: "I agree with your opening observations. Prices are increasing in both of the major markets that we serve, agricultural equipment and over-the-road transportation. As we are all aware, we either presently provide or are able to provide on short notice three major products to the agricultural equipment industry: valve bodies, axle housings, and differential cases. Based on the marketing research data that I have reviewed and talking with others in our trade association, I believe that we can expect to see a 5 percent increase in prices for these segments of this industry.

"On the other hand, the general price increase expected in the transportation industry is 6 percent. In this industry, we provide or are able to provide two major products: wheel hubs and brake calipers. These expected price increases will affect the **contribution** of these parts. I have prepared slides that reflect both present and proposed part contributions."

Table 11.2 Present Part Contribution with Existing Prices

	Valve Body	Axle Housing	Differential Case	Wheel Hub	Brake Caliper
Selling price	$40.00	$42.50	$30.00	$35.00	$40.00
Variable cost	$25.00	$20.00	$20.00	$17.50	$21.00
Contribution	$15.00	$22.50	$10.00	$17.50	$19.00

"Likewise, the proposed part contributions with anticipated price increases are found on the next slide."

Table 11.3 Proposed Part Contributions with a 5 Percent Price Increase for the Valve Body, Axle Housing, and Differential Case, and with a 6 Percent Increase for the Wheel Hub and Brake Caliper

	Valve Body	Axle Housing	Differential Case	Wheel Hub	Brake Caliper
Selling price	$42.00	$44.62	$31.50	$37.10	$42.40
Variable cost	$25.00	$20.00	$20.00	$17.50	$21.00
Contribution	$17.00	$24.62	$11.50	$19.60	$21.40

Now, in order to measure the impact, if any, of the proposed price increases, optimization technology would need to be employed. The objective would be contribution maximization incorporating the new part contributions reflected in Table 11.3. The routing matrix and departmental capacities would remain unchanged at present. The resulting contribution would, therefore, measure only the impact of the proposed price increases. The objective becomes:

Maximize $17.00(valve body) + $24.62(axle housing) + $11.50(differential case + $19.60(wheel hub) + $21.40(brake caliper)

(Subject to the product routings and departmental capacities in Table 2.4 [p. 16].)

Table 11.4 Maximum Contribution Considering the Effect of Price Increases

Objective: **Maximize Contribution**					
Product	Qty.	Department	Hrs. Required	Slack	Opportunity
Valve bodies	0	Core	200	0	$10.04
Axle housing	160	Assembly	80	120	0
Differential cases	0	Molding	200	0	$33.18
Wheel hubs	240	Cleaning	136	64	0
Brake calipers	0	Grinding	96	104	0
Totals	400		712	288	
Maximum contribution possible $8,643					

The projected price increases would provide incremental monthly contribution of $843 ($8,643 proposed – $7,800 benchmark). At this stage, the proposed product mix remained the same as the benchmark mix, due in part to the fact that the routing data set as well as departmental capacities had not as yet changed. If, however, the price increases had significantly affected the relative desirability of the parts, the mix would have been changed also.

The planning process was on its way.

Measuring the Impact of Variable Cost Increases

Next, Mr. Porter directed his attention to Jim and asked him what he saw in the way of cost increases for the coming year.

Jim replied: "We are expecting increases in all three categories of our variable costs, i.e., raw materials, labor, and energy. I have been working closely with our materials manager, and she advises me of the following expected increases:

1. Raw materials 6 percent.
2. Energy 30 percent.

"And, as we all know, the projected overall labor rate increase is 8 percent. I'll address them one at a time."

Jim used as his base the product material costs from Table 4.10 (p. 43) and incorporated the estimated increase of 6 percent.

Table 11.5 Calculation of Each Part's Proposed Material Costs

Product	Present Material Cost	6% Increase	Proposed Material Cost
Valve bodies	$ 2.50	$.15	$ 2.65
Axle housings	$ 4.00	$.24	$ 4.24
Differential cases	$ 6.00	$.36	$ 6.36
Wheel hubs	$ 7.00	$.42	$ 7.42
Brake calipers	$10.50	$.63	$11.13

He continued: "Even though energy costs are equal to an amount approximating just 5 percent of our material costs, their projected increase of 30 percent makes them worthy of consideration."

Table 11.6 Projected Product Energy Costs

Product	Proposed Material Cost	Energy Cost = 5% Material Cost	Increase of 30%
Valve bodies	$ 2.65	$.1325	$.04
Axle housings	$ 4.24	$.212	$.06
Differential cases	$ 6.36	$.318	$.10
Wheel hubs	$ 7.42	$.371	$.11
Brake calipers	$11.13	$.5565	$.17

The next item was the labor cost. The estimated increase in the cost of labor was 8 percent. To calculate the effect of the labor rate increase required the examination of each product's total processing time per the routing matrix originally presented as Table 2.4. If the molding machine crew's wages were fixed, their increase in pay would be reflected in the monthly fixed cost.

Jim continued: "Considering that the present labor rate is $10.00 per hour, an 8 percent increase would result in an $.80 increase per processing hour. We could apply this increase to each product based on its routing.

Table 11.7 Calculation of Each Part's Increase in Labor Cost

	Valve Body	Axle Housing	Differential Case	Wheel Hub	Brake Caliper
Processing time	2.0 hrs.	2.5 hrs.	1.0 hr.	1.3 hrs.	3.5 hrs.
$.80 increase in hourly rate	$1.60	$2.00	$.80	$1.04	$2.80

"Now we can determine the projected increase in each part's variable cost by summing the three components, i.e., material, energy, and labor. We can also determine each part's proposed variable cost for the planning period."

Table 11.8 Determination of Each Product's New Variable Cost

	Valve Body	Axle Housing	Differential Case	Wheel Hub	Brake Caliper
Increase in material cost	$ .15	$ .24	$ .36	$ .42	$ .63
Increase in energy cost	$ .04	$ .06	$ .10	$ .11	$ .17
Increase in labor cost	$ 1.60	$ 2.00	$ .80	$ 1.04	$ 2.80
Total variable cost increase	$ 1.79	$ 2.40	$ 1.26	$ 1.57	$ 3.60
Present part variable cost	$25.00	$20.00	$20.00	$17.50	$21.00
Proposed part variable cost	$26.79	$22.40	$21.26	$19.07	$24.60

Variable Cost Increases Are Measured Relative to Their Impact on Product Contributions

With the newly determined part variable costs and the new selling prices, per Table 11.3, the projected product contributions for the planning period could be determined. By injecting the new contributions into the objective for the algorithm, the impact of production cost increases could be measured.

Table 11.9 Determination of New Part Contributions Based on New Selling Prices and New Variable Costs

	Valve Body	Axle Housing	Differential Case	Wheel Hub	Brake Caliper
New selling prices (Table 11.3)	$42.00	$44.62	$31.50	$37.10	$42.40
New variable costs (Table 11.8)	$26.79	$22.40	$21.26	$19.07	$24.60
New contributions	$15.21	$22.22	$10.24	$18.03	$17.80

The objective for contribution maximization becomes:

Maximize **$15.21(valve body) + $22.22(axle housing) + $10.24(differential case) + $18.03(wheel hub) + $17.80(brake caliper)**

(Subject to product routings and departmental capacities in Table 2.4.)

Table 11.10 Maximum Contribution with New Selling Prices and New Variable Costs

Objective: **Maximize Contribution**					
Product	Qty.	Department	Hrs. Required	Slack	Opportunity
Valve bodies	0	Core	200	0	$8.38
Axle housings	160	Assembly	80	120	0
Differential cases	0	Molding	200	0	$31.03
Wheel hubs	240	Cleaning	136	64	0
Brake calipers	0	Grinding	96	104	0
Totals	400		712	288	
Maximum possible contribution $7,883					

Jim concluded: "The advantage of higher prices is nearly wiped out with the increased production costs. The detrimental effect of production cost increases is $760 per month ($8,643 from Table 11.4 − $7,883). Our net advantage thus far, considering both price increases and production cost increases, is just $83 per month ($7,883 − $7,800 benchmark)."

They wrapped up the initial part of the aggregate planning session and prepared to pick up the next day by considering the impact of improved operations. The next day they would consider the impact of incorporating several lean activities into the aggregate planning process. They realized that the initially recommended product mix reflected in Table 11.10 was subject to change as the operational improvements were considered.

Summary—Key Points

This chapter introduced the following ideas:

- The aggregate planning process is much easier using optimization techniques.
- The ability to predict results relies on internal manufacturing strengths as well as external market factors.
- The significance of price increases is not reflected in increased total revenue.
- The significance of variable cost increases is not reflected in total plant cost.
- Rather, the significance of price and cost increases is found in the effect such increases have on part contributions that constitute the major input to the optimization algorithm.
- Optimization technology users consider total revenue to be a by-product of the annual planning process and definitely not a beginning input.

CHAPTER 12

Incorporating Lean Manufacturing Activities (and Other Operational Improvements) into the Aggregate Plan

As the previous chapter considered the effect of price and cost changes, this chapter will focus on the effects (if any) of operational improvements on the aggregate planning process. Not all operational improvements produce financial improvements. In addition, the measurement of such improvements was previously elusive at best. This chapter will focus on routings and capacities.

Chapter Contents

- Measuring the financial impact of process improvements
- Measuring the financial impact of preventive maintenance
- Measuring the financial impact of reduced setup times
- Recognizing and measuring the impact of a market constraint
- Rethinking marketing's objective
- Political expediency may be very costly
- Summarizing the forecasting and budgeting process
- Expressing the results of constraint exploitation in primary financial measures

The second day of the aggregate planning process was about to begin. Mr. Porter began by asking Stephanie if some of the projects that they had been working on in operations will translate into increased profitability? She replied: "Yes, I believe they will. I've been working on several areas that I believe will show substantial improvements in profit. We have reduced process times by 20 percent on all jobs in the core department. We also have reduced the cycle time on the molding machine by 10 percent.

"I'm most proud, however, of the work done in the areas of preventive maintenance (PM) and setup time reductions. Our effective PM program has improved our runtime in molding so that we can operate an additional 40 hours per month. In addition, reduced setup times in both the core and molding departments will provide an additional 25 hours runtime in core and 20 hours more in molding."

Stephanie continued her presentation by reviewing the original product routing matrix presented as Table 2.4 (p. 16) and reproduced here as Table 12.1.

Table 12.1 Existing Product Routing Matrix

Department	Valve Body	Axle Housing	Differential Case	Wheel Hub	Brake Caliper	Time Available
Core	.4	.8	.1	.3	.9	200 hrs.
Assembly	.7	.2	.1	.2	.7	200 hrs.
Molding	.5	.5	.5	.5	.5	200 hrs.
Cleaning	.1	.7	.2	.1	.6	200 hrs.
Grinding	.3	.3	.1	.2	.8	200 hrs.

The next step for Stephanie was to incorporate the process time improvements into the routing matrix. She wanted to evaluate the impact of process improvements, the additional time provided by the preventive maintenance program, and the impact of improved setup times separately.

Measuring the Financial Impact of Process Improvements

The routing matrix in Table 12.1 was amended to incorporate the 20 percent improvement of process times in the core department and the 10 percent reduction of the molding machine cycle time.

Table 12.2 Routing Matrix Reflecting Process Time Improvements for Both Core and Molding

Department	Valve Body	Axle Housing	Differential Case	Wheel Hub	Brake Caliper	Time Available
Core	.32	.64	.08	.24	.72	200 hrs.
Molding	.45	.45	.45	.45	.45	200 hrs.

The objective for contribution maximization remained:

Maximize $15.21(valve body) + $22.22(axle housing) + $10.24(differential case) + $18.03(wheel hub) + $17.80(brake caliper)

(Subject to the product routings and departmental capacities in Tables 12.1 and 12.2.)

Table 12.3 Contribution with Reducing Core Process Times by 20 Percent and Reducing Molding Cycle Time by 10 Percent

Objective: **Maximize Contribution**

Product	Qty.	Department	Hrs. Required	Slack	Opportunity
Valve bodies	0	Core	200	0	$10.48
Axle housings	233	Assembly	89	111	0
Differential cases	0	Molding	200	0	$34.48
Wheel hubs	211	Cleaning	184	16	0
Brake calipers	0	Grinding	112	88	0
Totals	444		785	215	
Maximum contribution possible $8,982					

Stephanie continued: "As you can see, contribution has increased $1,099 from $7,883 (in Table 11.10) to the present $8,982. I really believe that this is very significant because this improvement is more than the $843 increase realized with a 5 percent and 6 percent price increase, (illustrated in Table 11.4, p. 120). The contribution provided from these two process improvements allows for 44 more molds as well as a significant movement in the ratio of wheel hubs to axle housings."

Measuring the Financial Impact of Preventive Maintenance

Mr. Porter was anxious to see the results of her preventive maintenance program. Stephanie explained: "The benefits of this PM program are due nearly exclusively to the fact that the runtime of the molding machine has improved from 200 hours per month to 240 hours per month. Some may argue that the major benefit is the elimination of downtime. Actually, the increase in runtime and the decrease in downtime are, in essence, the same. The financial impact of the preventive maintenance program is really very easy to measure. Only one very small modification to the data set is required. Consider this slide of Table 12.2, reproduced here as Table 12.4 with the single change noted."

Table 12.4 Data Set Modification Reflecting the Additional 40 Hours Run Time Available in Molding Due to Preventive Maintenance Program

Department	Valve Body	Axle Housing	Differential Case	Wheel Hub	Brake Caliper	Time Available
Core	.32	.64	.08	.24	.72	200 hrs.
Molding	.45	.45	.45	.45	.45	240 hrs.

The algorithm is activated for contribution maximization as the objective subject to product routings and departmental capacities per Tables 2.4 and 12.4 and provides the following results:

Table 12.5 Maximum Contribution with 40 Additional Hours Runtime in the Molding Department Attributable to Preventive Maintenance Program

Objective: **Maximize Contribution**					
Product	Qty.	Department	Hrs. Required	Slack	Opportunity
Valve bodies	0	Core	200	0	$10.48
Axle housings	180	Assembly	107	93	0
Differential cases	0	Molding	240	0	$34.48
Wheel hubs	353	Cleaning	161	39	0
Brake calipers	0	Grinding	125	75	0
Totals	**533**		**833**	**207**	
Maximum contribution possible $10,364					

Stephanie continued: "Without the aid of optimization techniques I could not have possibly been able to quantify the financial impact of our preventive maintenance program. Now it is clear that this program adds $1,382 per month to our bottom line." ($10,364 per Table 12.5 – $8,982 from Table 12.3 = $1,382.)

Reuben commented that the proposed number of wheel hubs had increased to 353 per month. Mr. Porter asked if that was a problem for marketing.

Reuben wasn't sure and wanted to see where they would end up after Stephanie presented her remaining operations improvements.

Measuring the Financial Impact of Reduced Setup Times

Stephanie continued: "We have also been working diligently all of this past year to reduce our setup times. The benefits of these improvements include not only the increase in the runtimes in these two departments, but allows us to better synchronize the flow through the plant, which will enhance our customer service objectives. We have made tremendous strides in both of our constrained departments, core and molding. Now it's time to measure the financial impact of the setup time improvements in terms of the additional runtime provided. I'll restate Table 12.4 to reflect these modifications to the data set, which includes 25 more runtime hours for core and 20 more runtime hours for molding."

Table 12.6 Data Set Modifications Reflecting Runtime Additions Made Possible with Reduced Setup Times in the Core and Molding Departments

Department	Valve Body	Axle Housing	Differential Case	Wheel Hub	Brake Caliper	Time Available
Core	.32	.64	.08	.24	.72	225 hrs.
Molding	.45	.45	.45	.45	.45	260 hrs.

The algorithm was activated again with the objective of contribution maximization subject to the product routings and departmental capacities per Tables 12.1 and 12.6. The results are presented as Table 12.7.

Table 12.7 Maximum Contribution with Runtime Improvements in Both the Core and Molding Departments Attributable to Reduced Setup Times

Objective: **Maximize Contribution**					
Product	**Qty.**	**Department**	**Hrs. Required**	**Slack**	**Opportunity**
Valve bodies	0	Core	225	0	$10.48
Axle housings	215	Assembly	116	84	0
Differential cases	0	Molding	260	0	$34.48
Wheel hubs	362	Cleaning	187	13	0
Brake calipers	0	Grinding	137	63	0
Totals	577		925	160	
Maximum contribution possible $11,326					

There was no doubt about it. Stephanie was the hero in this planning and budgeting session. The financial impact from reduced setup times was clearly a significant $962 per month ($11,326 − $10,364, per Table 12.5).

Mr. Porter noted that the most subtle operations improvements had contributed the most to the bottom line. These operational improvements included:

1. Process time improvements.
2. Runtime improvements attributable to effective preventive maintenance.
3. Runtime improvements attributable to setup time reductions.

The common thread of these operational improvements was that they were all directed exclusively to *constrained* departments. Mr. Porter said: "What Stephanie and the other operations people have done are certainly productive improvements, and the financial impact is tremendous. Previously, such activities were considered to be intangible and their impact impossible to measure. Now, not only can we measure them, we have learned that such activities have a profound effect on plant profitability.

"Let's summarize the major factors that have affected our proposed forecast and budget for next year. We'll begin with the $7,800 contribution benchmark presented in Table 11.1 (p. 119) and work up to the $11,326 in Table 12.7."

Table 12.8 Individual Item and Cumulative Effect of Planning and Budgeting Items

Planning Item	Financial Impact	Location	Cumulative Contribution
Beginning point		Table 11.1	$ 7,800
Selling price increases	+$843	Table 11.4	$ 8,643
Production cost increases	−$760	Table 11.10	$ 7,883
Process time improvements	+$1,099	Table 12.3	$ 8,982
Runtime improvements due to preventive maintenance	+$1,382	Table 12.5	$10,364
Runtime improvements due to reduced setup times	+$962	Table 12.7	$11,326
Totals	$3,526		$11,326

Mr. Porter commented: "That's great! This has been the most unique planning session that I have ever participated in, however, I would be naïve if I thought that $11,326 would be our final contribution plan."

Recognizing and Measuring the Impact of a Market Constraint

"Reuben, you had some hesitation as the number of wheel hubs in our optimum product mix continued to increase. What seems to be the problem?"

Reuben believed the market could bear more than 300 wheel hubs, especially at the new price of $37.10 developed in Table 11.3 (p. 120). He thought that they should plan for a total of 300 per month.

Mr. Porter reminded them to be realistic: "We will need to determine what that action will cost us, however. We all know that any restriction to the data set will reduce the contribution. The solution is very simple. All we need to do is add a simple modification to the objective, specifying a limit of wheel hubs to 300."

Wheel hubs ≤ 300

The contribution maximization objective would be:

Maximize $15.21 (valve body) + $22.22 (axle housing) + $10.24 (differential case) + $18.03 (wheel hubs) + $17.80 (brake caliper)

(Subject to product routings and departmental capacities in Table 12.9.)

Table 12.9 Product Routing Matrix Reflecting Process Time Improvements, and the Additional Runtimes Made Available Due to Preventive Maintenance and Setup Time Reductions

Department	Valve Body	Axle Housing	Differential Case	Wheel Hub	Brake Caliper	Time Available
Core	.32	.64	.08	.24	.72	225 hrs.
Assembly	.7	.2	.1	.2	.7	200 hrs.
Molding	.45	.45	.45	.45	.45	260 hrs.
Cleaning	.1	.7	.2	.1	.6	200 hrs.
Grinding	.3	.3	.1	.2	.8	200 hrs.

The new contribution reflecting the restriction of wheel hub sales is presented in Table 12.10.

Table 12.10 Maximum Contribution When Wheel Hubs Are Limited to 300

Objective: **Maximize Contribution**					
Product	Qty.	Department	Hrs. Required	Slack	Opportunity
Valve bodies	7	Core	225	0	$20.93
Axle housings	230	Assembly	115	85	0
Differential cases	40	Molding	260	0	$18.80
Wheel hubs	300	Cleaning	200	0	$.52
Brake calipers	0	Grinding	135	65	0
Total	577		935	150	
Maximum contribution possible $11,036					

The limiting of wheel hubs had a profound effect on the product mix and resulting contribution. The limitation reduced total contribution $290 ($11,326, per Table 12.7 – $11,036).

Rethinking Marketing's Objective

Reuben went on to say: "I used to chase revenue when my commission was based on total sales. In fact, with the new selling prices, we could generate $22,947 total revenue with the product mix in Table 12.10 when contribution is maximized at $11,036. However, using the same data set but setting revenue maximization as the objective, we could generate $23,632 in revenue but contribution would only be $10,707."

Mr. Porter agreed, saying, "Beginning with the new planning period, let's consider basing your incentive pay on how close you come to achieving the optimum product mix that generates maximum contribution. We'll let revenue maximization go by the wayside, along with overhead absorption."

Political Expediency May Be Very Costly

"I have a friend who runs a plant in North Carolina. It would really help him out if we could provide him with 50 brake calipers per month. Let's see what that would cost. If the cost is significant, I'll just tell him that we're not in a position to do that."

So with contribution maximization as the objective and using Table 12.9 as plant routings and departmental capacities, the team activated the algorithm and got the following results.

Table 12.11 Maximum Contribution If Providing Friend 50 Brake Calipers Per Month

Objective: **Maximize Contribution**					
Product	**Qty.**	**Department**	**Hrs. Required**	**Slack**	**Opportunity**
Valve bodies	0	Core	225	0	$21.39
Axle housings	176	Assembly	135	65	0
Differential cases	51	Molding	260	0	$18.95
Wheel hubs	300	Cleaning	194	6	0
Brake calipers	50	Grinding	158	42	0
Totals	**577**		**972**	**113**	
Maximum contribution possible $10,732					

They all realized that this would definitely not be a good decision. Actually, they already knew that but didn't realize its magnitude. This decision would cost OpTek $304 per month. Political expediency can be very costly. Now OpTek had the means to *measure the cost of doing counterproductive things*. Mr. Porter quickly dismissed the thought of providing the brake calipers to his friend.

Summarizing the Forecasting and Budgeting Process

Mr. Porter explained that the monthly contribution of $11,036 was the maximum that could be achieved within their constraint set, which included both market and production constraints: "This is our contribution opportunity with constraint exploitation. Our final forecast and manufacturing budget cannot be completed without the input from the capital budget. Our capital budget will not be limited to facilitating our marketing and manufacturing plans and budgets, but will assist in their definition. The final form of our market and production plan must include the benefits afforded by our capital plan. Our marketing, production, and capital plans are not mutually exclusive. They are totally integrative and provide a great amount of synergy relative to profit generation. It involves the management of constraints at its best. The $11,036 contribution opportunity achieved with constraint exploitation becomes the primary input for the capital planning process."

Expressing the Results of Constraint Exploitation in Primary Financial Measures

Jim had also provided their proposed monthly fixed cost plan/budget. Fixed manufacturing overhead would be budgeted at $5,400, and OpTek's predominant production constraint was still the molding department. Molding production, however, would now be planned at 577 molds monthly (260 available hours ÷ .45 hours per mold = 577 molds) due to the operational improvements achieved in that area. He said: "Now we are ready to calculate our projected productivity of capital, ROI, and break-even level achieved via constraint exploitation."

$$\frac{\text{Monthly net}}{\text{operating profit}} = \$11,036 \text{ contribution} - \$5,400 \text{ fixed cost} = \$5,636$$

$$\textbf{Capital Productivity: } \frac{\text{Ending assets}}{\text{Beginning assets}} = \frac{\text{Output}}{\text{Input}} = \frac{\$501,232^*}{\$433,600} = \textbf{1.156}$$

*Beginning $433,600 + (12 \times \$5,636) = \$501,232$

$$\textbf{ROI: } \frac{\text{Ending assets} - \text{Beginning assets}}{\text{Beginning assets}} = \frac{\text{Profit}}{\text{Beginning assets}} = \frac{\$67,632}{\$433,600} = \textbf{15.6\%}$$

Break-Even Level

$$\frac{\text{Monthly contribution}}{\text{Monthly molds}} = \frac{\$11,036}{577} = \$19.13 \text{ contribution per mold}$$

$$\frac{\text{Total monthly fixed cost}}{\text{Contribution per mold}} = \frac{\$5,400}{\$19.13} = 282 \text{ molds to break even}$$

$$\frac{\text{Molds to break even}}{\text{Total molds made}} = \frac{282}{577} = \textbf{48.9\%} \text{ molding capacity to break even}$$

Commenting on the great progress they had made in only one year, Mr. Porter said: "Doing effective things is really paying off in a big way. Let's get together at the same place and same time next week to complete the planning process as we develop our capital budget. We really have some great opportunities for departmental expansion."

Summary—Key Points

In this chapter we have learned that:

- Seemingly intangible operating improvements, i.e., preventive maintenance, can be translated into tangible financial results.
- If any operating improvement can be expressed in *any* of the following three terms, the improvement can be incorporated into the optimization algorithm and the financial impact measured:
  1. Variable cost change for any part that translates directly into that part's contribution.
  2. Routing changes.
  3. Departmental capacity.
- The performance measure and subsequent incentive for the marketing manager should be redirected from total sales to meeting the contribution maximizing product mix.
- The results of constraint exploitation should be analyzed in primary financial measures.

CHAPTER 13

Capital Budgeting
Is Just One Step
in a Seamless Process

This chapter will address the capital budgeting portion of the aggregate planning process. In the previous two chapters we addressed the marketing and operational aspects of the aggregate planning process. We formulated the initial aggregate plan by exploiting the basic production constraints, i.e., core and molding.

The capital budgeting portion of the aggregate plan picks up where the marketing and operations plans leave off. The production constraints have been *exploited* as a result of the marketing and operations plans. Now it is time to consider the financial impact of *elevating* those constraints.

Chapter Contents

- The annual capital budgeting process begins where the marketing and manufacturing plans leave off
- Other information requirements to complete the capital planning process
- Capital projects are evaluated relative to their ability to generate incremental contribution
- Measuring the financial benefits of elevating the core constraint
- Measuring the financial benefits of elevating the molding constraint
- The capital planning process may suggest further changes to the product mix

The capital portion of the aggregate plan should be considered the latter part of a seamless planning and budgeting process. This part of the budgeting process should assist in the final definition of the marketing and manufacturing plans. The recommended marketing mix coming out of the capital planning session will in all likelihood be substantially different than at the beginning of the process.

The Annual Capital Budgeting Process Begins Where the Marketing and Manufacturing Plans Leave Off

OpTek can now begin work on its capital budget inasmuch as the initial marketing forecast and operating budget, which maximized contribution *within their constraints*, has been completed. The starting point for the capital budget will be the statistics associated with the planned optimum product mix attained within their constraints, reproduced here as Table 13.1.

Table 13.1 Optimum Product Mix and Maximum Contribution for OpTek Prior to Capital Additions/Improvements

Product	Qty.	Department	Hrs. Required	Slack	Opportunity
Valve bodies	7	Core	225	0	$20.93
Axle housings	230	Assembly	115	85	0
Differential cases	40	Molding	260	0	$18.80
Wheel hubs	300	Cleaning	200	0	$ .52
Brake calipers	0	Grinding	135	65	0
Totals	577		935	150	
Maximum contribution possible $11,036					

Not only does Table 13.1 summarize the marketing plan at this stage of the process, it provides projected monthly department loading requirements. More importantly, this product mix plan highlights the production constraints that will restrict further profit generation. Last, this table summarizes OpTek's monthly financial expectations, i.e., Contribution = Total revenue – Variable cost of sales and serves not only as a planning tool but also as a summary income statement monitor.

Other Information Requirements to Complete the Capital Planning Process

There are several other items of information that are required in order to complete the capital plan, i.e., the newly developed product contributions, the product routings and existing departmental capacities that form the data set to arrive at Table 13.1, and, of course, the capital cost of additional and replacement equipment.

Table 13.2 Product Contributions Based on Selling Prices and Variable Costs Developed During the Initial Stages of the Planning Process

	Valve Body	Axle Housing	Differential Case	Wheel Hub	Brake Caliper
New contribution	$15.21	$22.22	$10.24	$18.03	$17.80

The next item of information needed to develop the capital budget is the product routing matrix and departmental capacities.

Table 13.3 Product Routing Matrix and Departmental Capacities to Support the Optimum Product Mix Developed During the Initial Marketing and Operations Planning Process

Department	Valve Body	Axle Housing	Differential Case	Wheel Hub	Brake Caliper	Monthly Capacity
Core	.32	.64	.08	.24	.72	225 hrs.
Assembly	.7	.2	.1	.2	.7	200 hrs.
Molding	.45	.45	.45	.45	.45	260 hrs.
Cleaning	.1	.7	.2	.1	.6	200 hrs.
Grinding	.3	.3	.1	.2	.8	200 hrs.

The staff now was ready to review the capital requests that had been submitted. There were, in fact, three capital requests waiting for review:

1. **Request for additional core equipment**
   a. This equipment would be tooled to process the parts in the agricultural equipment line. This equipment would process valve bodies, axle housings, and differential cases.
   b. The advantage of this equipment would be reduced process times. This new equipment could reduce process times on the above-mentioned products by 30 percent.
   c. The equipment could operate 180 hours per month.
   d. The capital cost of the equipment is $40,000.

2. Request for a new molding machine

a. The proposed molding equipment would have the same performance specifications as the existing molding equipment.

b. The machine would provide an additional 180 operating hours per month.

c. The purpose of this equipment would be exclusively to relieve the molding constraint.

d. The capital cost of the new molding machine is $80,000.

3. Request for a new grinding machine

a. This proposed equipment would replace the existing worn out equipment.

b. The new equipment could be operated 200 hour per month and provide reduced process times on all parts by 15 percent.

c. The capital cost for this replacement equipment is $20,000.

OpTek did not have capital limitations, but it was required to maintain at least an overall plant ROI of 15 percent. This was the challenge before the staff.

Capital Projects Are Evaluated Relative to Their Ability to Generate Incremental Contribution

The approach to evaluate capital requests is very straightforward. It begins with determining the expected cash flow to be provided by the proposed equipment. This step is accomplished by initially expressing the equipment's operating benefits in the routing and capacity matrix. Then the new projected plant contribution is determined using contribution maximization as the objective for the algorithm. The projected contribution is then compared with the contribution without the equipment. The difference is the cash flow associated with the proposed equipment.

Measuring the Financial Benefits of Elevating the Core Constraint

The team began with the proposed core equipment. The operating benefits can be expressed very simply by modifying the routing matrix presented in Table 13.3.

Table 13.4 Revised Routing Matrix Incorporating Benefits of New Core Equipment
i.e., 30 Percent Reduction in Process Time for the Valve Body, Axle
Housing, and Differential Case (Wheel Hubs and Brake Calipers Would
Continue to be Routed Through the Existing Core Equipment)

Department	Valve Body	Axle Housing	Differential Case	Wheel Hub	Brake Caliper	Monthly Capacity
Core (existing)	.32	.64	.08	.24	.72	225 hrs.
Core (proposed)	.224	.448	.056	0	0	180 hrs.

The three products that would benefit from reduced process times would simultaneously benefit from reduced variable costs and increased contributions.

Table 13.5 Calculation of Core Labor Cost Reduction from New Core Equipment

Present core labor cost for valve bodies	= .32 hrs. × $10.80	= $3.456
Proposed core labor cost	= .224 hrs. × $10.80	= $2.419
	Savings	$1.037
Present core labor cost for axle housings	= .64 hrs. × $10.80	= $6.912
Proposed core labor cost	= .448 hrs. × $10.80	= $4.838
	Savings	$2.074
Present core labor cost for differential cases	= .08 hrs. × $10.80	= $ .864
Proposed core labor cost	= .056 hrs. × $10.80	= $ .605
	Savings	$ .259

The labor cost reductions in Table 13.5 will likewise be reflected as increased part contributions.

Table 13.6 Calculation of Proposed Part Contributions with Proposed New Core Equipment

	Valve Body	Axle Housing	Differential Case
Contribution present	$15.21	$22.22	$10.24
Labor savings	$ 1.04	$ 2.07	$ .26
Contribution proposed	$16.25	$24.29	$10.50

With the above information, the operating cash flow to be expected from the proposed new core equipment could be calculated. The objective for contribution maximization became:

Maximize $16.25(valve body) + $24.29(axle housing) + $10.50(differential case) +$18.03(wheel hubs) + $17.80(brake caliper)

(Subject to product routings and departmental capacities in Tables 13.3 and 13.4.)

They had also remembered to include the market constraint that developed during the marketing and manufacturing planning process.

Wheel hubs ≤ 300

Table 13.7 Maximum Contribution with Proposed Core Equipment

Objective: **Maximize Contribution**					
Product	**Qty.**	**Department**	**Hrs. Required**	**Slack**	**Opportunity**
Valve bodies	40	Core (existing)	72	153	0
		Core (proposed)	117	63	0
Axle housings	237	Assembly	136	64	0
Differential cases	0	Molding	260	0	$33.13
Wheel hubs	300	Cleaning	200	0	$13.40
Brake calipers	0	Grinding	143	57	0
Totals	**577**		**928**	**337**	
Maximum contribution possible: $11,816					

Therefore, the cash flow for this proposal was $780 per month, or $9,360 per year ($11,816 per Table 13.7 – the $11,036 benchmark per Table 13.1).

The nondiscounted total system ROI after this proposed investment was 16.3 percent, calculated as follows:

Table 13.8 System ROI with Proposed Core Equipment

Total annual contribution = $11,816 × 12		= $141,792
Less annual fixed cost = $5,400 × 12		= $ 64,800
Net operating profit		= $ 76,992
Total system **ROI** =	$\dfrac{\text{Net operating profits}}{\text{Total assets}}$ = $\dfrac{\$76,992}{\$473,600^*}$	= **16.3%**

Beginning $433,600 + $40,000 cost of core equipment = $473,600.

OpTek noted that the proposed core equipment would be a qualifying investment inasmuch as total system ROI of 16.3 percent after the investment would exceed the required hurdle rate of 15 percent.

Measuring the Financial Benefits of Elevating the Molding Constraint

Now it was time to consider the proposal of adding a new molding machine. This machine had no performance advantages over the existing molding machine. The new machine would be strictly used to relieve the existing molding constraint by providing an additional 180 operating hours. The benefits of this proposal can be expressed with a single line-item change in the data set, as shown.

Table 13.9 Amended Routing Matrix Reflecting the Addition of 180 Operating Hours to Molding Capacity

	Valve Body	Axle Housing	Differential Case	Wheel Hub	Brake Caliper	**Monthly Capacity**
Molding (existing)	.45	.45	.45	.45	.45	260 hrs.
Molding (proposed)	.45	.45	.45	.45	.45	440 hrs.

The contribution objective uses the part contributions presented in Table 13.2. This procedure allows the evaluation of each proposal based on its own merits without, as in the present example, considering the advantages of the proposed core equipment:

Maximize $15.21(valve body) + $22.22(axle housing) + $10.24(differential case) + $18.03(wheel hub) + $17.80(brake caliper)

(Subject to the product routings and departmental capacities in Tables 13.3 and 13.9, and the marketing constraint for wheel hubs ≤ 300.)

Table 13.10 Maximum Contribution with a New Molding Machine

Objective: **Maximize Contribution**					
Product	**Qty.**	**Department**	**Hrs. Required**	**Slack**	**Opportunity**
Valve bodies	105	Core	202	23	0
Axle housings	90	Assembly	200	0	$11.88
Differential cases	482	Molding	440	0	10.52
Wheel hubs	300	Cleaning	200	0	21.58
Brake calipers	0	Grinding	167	33	0
Totals	**977**		**1,209**	**56**	
Maximum contribution possible $13,941					

With the determination of the projected contribution provided with the addition of a new molding machine, the projected total system ROI can be calculated.

Table 13.11 Projected System ROI with the New Molding Machine

Total annual projected contribution = $13,941 × 12	= $167,292
Less annual projected fixed cost = $5,400 × 12	= $ 64,800
Projected net operating profit	= $102,492
Total projected system ROI $= \dfrac{102,492}{\$513,600*} = 20.0\%$	

Beginning $433,600 + $80,000 cost of new molding machine = $513,600.

It was quickly noted that this proposal provided an excellent system ROI of 20.0 percent, which was substantially better than with the proposal to acquire new core equipment, i.e., 16.3 percent.

The Capital Planning Process May Suggest Further Changes to the Product Mix

Reuben also noted the major change in the proposed product mix (revealed in Table 13.10). The addition of the 180 hours of molding capacity provided for 400 more molds, which would be utilized predominantly for differential cases, which had the lowest of all individual part contributions. This proposal would suggest that they should move substantially away from axle housings and toward differential cases. Reuben wasn't altogether comfortable with that prospect at this stage.

As the aggregate planning process progresses through the initial stages of the capital portion, it becomes clear that the aggregate planning process is very dynamic.

Summary—Key Points

Aggregate planning is a dynamic process. This chapter illustrates clearly that:

- Using optimization techniques reveals that the plan is being defined as the planning process unfolds.
- The capital portion of the process is not the means to facilitate the aggregate plan; it simply assists in defining the aggregate plan.
- The final form of the aggregate plan will, therefore, provide the plant with the maximum possible profit within its manufacturing capability and marketing constraints.
- The capital planning process can suggest further changes to the product mix.

CHAPTER 14

Finalizing the Aggregate Planning Process

This chapter will illustrate the final stages of the aggregate planning process.

By incorporating optimization technology, the finalized aggregate plan will generate the maximum possible total plant contribution considering both the manufacturing capabilities of the plant and any projected marketing constraints. The final version of the optimized aggregate plan incorporates:

1. Price and cost increases.
2. Operational improvements.
3. Elevation of major production constraints.

It should be noted that a plant can optimize its aggregate planning process even if it cannot for any reason elevate its constraints. It would, in that case, be maximizing its plant contribution within its existing constraints.

Chapter Contents:

- The capital planning process may reveal additional constraints
- The financial impact of nonstandard processes
- Measuring the financial impact of replacement equipment
- Measuring the synergistic effect of implementing capital proposals simultaneously
- The primary financial measures for the aggregate plan
- Measuring the financial impact of a marketing constraint

As mentioned in the previous chapter, the aggregate planning process is very dynamic and each stage of the process optimizes the projected plant contribution up through that stage.

The Capital Planning Process May Reveal Additional Constraints

At the end of the previous planning session, Stephanie noted that the cleaning department emerged as the major constraint, with the highest opportunity of $21.58. Inasmuch as the opportunity was an indication of the relative financial benefit of elevating the constraint, they discussed the possibility of increasing cleaning capacity.

The Financial Impact of Nonstandard Processes

Stephanie remembered that they had replaced their cleaning equipment several years ago with new equipment. Their old equipment, although deactivated, was still on the premises. She thought: We could reinstall the old equipment and retool it to process the projected large number of differential cases and set it up next to the other cleaning equipment to help relieve the cleaning constraint. The only problem is that the old equipment is slower and because of its age requires more maintenance.

Stephanie checked her records, which revealed that the routing for the differential cases on the old cleaning equipment was .25 hours compared to the present .2 hours with the newer equipment. She told the others: "That would add $.54 to the variable cost of the differential case (.05 hour × $10.80 = $.54) and reduce its contribution to $9.70 ($10.24 − $.54 = $9.70). In addition, because of the condition of the old equipment and its maintenance requirements, we would only be able to run that equipment for 150 hours per month."

Right away, Jim balked at using a nonstandard, more expensive process in the plant. He thought that couldn't be a productive thing to do. Mr. Porter prevailed, however, and they prepared to simulate the reactivation of the old, less efficient, more costly machine.

They observed that the need for more cleaning capacity didn't become a priority until after they had considered adding 180 hours to molding capacity. So the routing matrix as presented in Table 13.3 was modified to reflect 440 hours of molding capacity *plus* the following change representing the use of the old cleaning equipment to process differential cases.

Table 14.1 Routing Matrix Modification to Reflect Old Cleaning Equipment to Process Differential Cases

Department	Valve Body	Axle Housing	Differential Case	Wheel Hub	Brake Caliper	Monthly Capacity
Cleaning (existing equipment)	.1	.7	0	.1	.6	200 hrs.
Cleaning (old equipment)	0	0	.25	0	0	150 hrs.

The objective for contribution maximization became:

Maximize $15.21(valve body) + $22.22(axle housing) + $9.70(differential case) + $18.03wheel hub + $17.80(brake caliper)

(Subject to product routings and departmental capacities per Tables 13.3 [p. 139], 13.9, 14.1, and the marketing constraint for wheel hubs $\leq$ 300.)

Table 14.2 Maximum Contribution with New Molding Machine Plus Using Old, Slower, and More Costly Cleaning Equipment to Supplement the Cleaning Constraint

Objective: **Maximize Contribution**

Product	Qty.	Department	Hrs. Required	Slack	Opportunity
Valve bodies	98	Core	203	22	0
Axle housings	134	Assembly	200	0	$ .26
Differential cases	445	Molding	440	0	$17.53
Wheel hubs	300	Cleaning (existing)	134	66	0
Brake calipers	0	Cleaning (proposed)	111	39	0
		Grinding	174	26	0
Totals	977		1,262	153	
Maximum contribution possible $14,194					

Jim in particular was surprised to see that total contribution could be increased when using a more expensive nonstandard process in the plant. The reason was that the existing cleaning capacity would be constrained with a new molding machine and the benefits of the added capacity in cleaning outweighed the increase in the variable cost of the differential cases.

Measuring the Financial Impact of Replacement Equipment

Replacement grinding equipment would provide 200 hours of operation. These 200 hours were not additional but rather replacement hours. The replacement of the grinding equipment was a necessity because of its condition and not an option. The new equipment did, however, provide a 15 percent reduction in process times on all parts. The capital cost for the new grinding station was $20,000. The modifications to the routing matrix reflecting new replacement grinding equipment were as follows:

Table 14.3 Modifications to Routing Matrix and Resulting Cost Reductions Due to Proposed New Replacement Grinding Equipment

	Valve Body	Axle Housing	Differential Case	Wheel Hub	Brake Caliper	**Monthly Capacity**
Grinding (present)	.3	.3	.1	.2	.8	200 hrs.
Grinding (proposed)	.255	.255	.085	.17	.68	200 hrs.
Time savings	.045 hrs.	.045 hrs.	.015 hrs.	.03 hrs.	.12 hrs.	
Cost reduction	$.486	$.486	$.162	$.324	$1.30	

The modified product contributions reflecting the benefit provided by the replacement grinding equipment are presented in Table 14.4.

Table 14.4 Calculation of Proposed Product Contributions with Proposed Replacement Grinding Equipment

	Valve Body	**Axle Housing**	**Differential Case**	**Wheel Hub**	**Brake Caliper**
Contribution (present)	$15.21	$22.22	$10.24	$18.03	$17.80
Labor savings with replacement grinding equipment	$.49	$.49	.16	$.32	$1.30
Contribution (proposed)	$15.70	$22.71	$10.40	$18.35	$19.10

The projected operating cash flow associated with the acquisition of replacement grinding equipment could now be calculated. The objective for contribution maximization became:

Maximize $15.70(valve body) + $22.71(axle housing) + $10.40(differential case) + $18.35(wheel hub) + $19.10(brake caliper)

(Subject to product routings and departmental capacities per Tables 13.3 and 14.3 and the marketing constraint, i.e., wheel hubs ≤ 300.)

Table 14.5 Maximum Contribution with Replacement Grinding Equipment

Objective: **Maximize Contribution**					
Product	Qty.	Department	Hrs. Required	Slack	Opportunity
Valve bodies	77	Core	225	0	$21.91
Axle housings	200	Assembly	154	46	0
Differential cases	0	Molding	260	0	$19.31
Wheel hubs	300	Cleaning	178	22	0
Brake calipers	0	Grinding	122	78	0
Totals	577		939	146	
Maximum contribution possible $11,256					

The projected system ROI incorporating the replacement grinding equipment could be calculated:

Table 14.6 Projected System ROI with Replacement Grinding Equipment

Total annual projected contribution = $11,256 × 12	= $135,072
Less annual projected fixed cost = $5,400 × 12	= $ 64,800
Projected annual net operating profit	= $ 70,272
Total projected system ROI $= \dfrac{\$70,272}{\$453,600*} = 15.4\%$	

Beginning $433,600 + $20,000 cost of replacement grinding equipment

Measuring the Synergistic Effect of Implementing Capital Proposals Simultaneously

Mr. Porter wanted to wrap up the capital budgeting session so he instructed Jim to calculate the net cash flow and total system ROI incorporating all three capital proposals, including reactivating the old cleaning equipment.

Jim prepared a modified routing matrix incorporating all operational benefits provided by all of the proposed capital investment opportunities.

Table 14.7 Modified Routing Matrix Incorporating All Changes Resulting from Implementing All Three Requested Capital Projects Plus Reactivating the Old Cleaning Equipment

	\multicolumn{5}{c}{Combined Modified Routing Matrix}	
Department	Valve Body	Axle Housing	Differential Case	Wheel Hub	Brake Caliper	Time Available
Core (existing)	0	0	0	.24	.72	225 hrs.
Core (proposed)	.224	.448	.056	0	0	180 hrs.
Assembly	.7	.2	.1	.2	.7	200 hrs.
Molding (proposed)	.45	.45	.45	.45	.45	440 hrs.
Cleaning (existing)	.1	.7	0	.1	.6	200 hrs.
Cleaning (proposed)	0	0	.25	0	0	150 hrs.
Grinding (proposed)	.255	.255	.085	.17	.68	200 hrs.

Then Jim converted the operational improvements into financial terms, i.e., increased product contributions.

Table 14.8 Individual Product Contributions Incorporating All Operational Improvements Reflected in the Routing Matrix in Table 14.7

	Valve Body	Axle Housing	Differential Case	Wheel Hub	Brake Caliper
Present contribution (Table 13.2)	$15.21	$22.22	$10.24	$18.03	$17.80
Benefit of proposed core machine (Table 13.6)	$ 1.04	$ 2.07	$ .26	0	0
Benefit of proposed grinding machine (Table 14.3)	$ .49	$ .49	$ .16	$ .32	$ 1.30
Effect of using old cleaning equipment (Table 14.1)			($.54)		
Proposed contribution	$16.74	$24.78	$10.12	$18.35	$19.10

The basis for the integrated marketing, production, and financial plans, including the capital budget, is illustrated below with the contribution maximizing product mix:

Maximize $16.74(valve body) + $24.78(axle housing) + $10.12(differential case) + $18.35(wheel hub) + $19.10(brake caliper)

(Subject to the routing and departmental capacities in Table 14.7 and including the marketing constraint, i.e., wheel hubs ≤ 300.)

Table 14.9 Maximum Contribution and Resulting Product Mix When Incorporating All of the Modifications Required by the Capital Budget

Product	Qty.	Department	Hrs. Required	Slack	Opportunity
Valve bodies	82	Core (existing)	72	153	0
Axle housings	231	Core (proposed)	144	36	0
Differential cases	364	Assembly	200	0	$ 7.73
Wheel hubs	300	Molding (proposed)	440	0	$20.77
Brake calipers	0	Cleaning (existing)	200	0	$19.84
		Cleaning (proposed)	91	59	0
		Grinding (proposed)	162	38	0
Totals	**977**		**1,309**	**286**	
Maximum contribution possible $16,286					

With this information, Jim was able to calculate total system ROI resulting from incorporating the three capital proposals simultaneously.

Table 14.10 Total System ROI When Implementing All Three Capital Proposals Simultaneously

Total annual projected contribution = $16,286 × 12	= $195,432
Total annual projected fixed cost = $5,400 × 12	= $ 64,800
Total annual projected annual net operating profit	= $130,632
Total projected system ROI $= \dfrac{\text{Net operating profit}}{\text{Total assets}} = \dfrac{\$130,632}{\$573,600^*}$ **= 22.8%**	

*$433,600 beginning + $40,000 for core equipment + $80,000 for molding equipment + $20,000 for grinding equipment = $573,600.

Table 14.11 Summary Cash Flows and Ranking of the Three Capital Project Opportunities

Rankings of Capital Projects			
Project Description	*Net Cash Flow**	*Projected System ROI*	**Ranking**
Add core capacity	$ 9,360	16.3% per Table 13.8	3
Add molding capacity	$34,860	20.0% per Table 13.11	2
Add replacement grinding equipment	$ 2,640	15.4% per Table 14.6	4
Total capital budget	$63,000	22.8% per Table 14.10	1

*Net cash flow is determined by comparing the total contribution provided by each investment opportunity with the benchmark contribution of $11,036 in Table 13.1. For example, total contribution provided by adding core capacity per Table 13.7 is $11,816. Then $11,816 − $11,036 = $780 × 12 = $9,360.

Of particular interest to Jim was the fact that the net cash flow, when considering the total capital budget, exceeded the sum of the cash flows provided by the three individual investment opportunities. Likewise, the projected system ROI for the total capital budget exceeded all of the three projects when considered in isolation. This, he reasoned, illustrated the magnitude of the synergy involved when implementing multiple projects simultaneously.

They all studied Table 14.9 very carefully. Mr. Porter commented: "This will be a very ambitious plan. We had begun the planning process with 400 total molds per Table 11.1 (p. 119), and now, with the operational improvements combined with the benefits from the proposed capital plan, the total number of molds would be 977."

Of particular concern to Mr. Porter was Reuben's ability to sell the quantity and mix of products reflected in Table 14.9. However, Reuben confirmed: "The only restriction I can foresee is limiting wheel hubs to 300, which is incorporated into the final version of the overall plan. I am even becoming enthusiastic about entering the market for differential cases. I am still amazed that the marketing and manufacturing plan recommended 364 differential cases, more than any of the other products, considering that the differential cases had by far the lowest individual part contribution."

Individual Product Contributions
(from Table 14.8)

Product	Contribution	Ranking
Valve body	$16.74	4
Axle housing	$24.78	1
Differential case	**$10.12**	5
Wheel hub	$18.35	3
Brake caliper	$19.10	2

The Primary Financial Measures for the Aggregate Plan

Mr. Porter now wanted to express the results in their three primary financial measures, i.e., capital productivity, ROI, and break-even level, considering the implementation of the entire capital budget including the reactivation of the old cleaning equipment brought in from the "bone yard" to process differential cases. So they calculated OpTek's primary financial measures based on upon the implementation of the marketing, manufacturing, and capital plans:

$$\text{Monthly net operating profit} = \$16,286 \text{ contribution} - \$5,400 \text{ fixed cost} = \$10,886$$

And $10,886 \times 12 = $130,632 annual projected net operating profit

Capital Productivity: $\dfrac{\text{Ending assets}}{\text{Beginning assets}} = \dfrac{\text{Output}}{\text{Input}} = \dfrac{\$704,232^*}{\$573,600} = \mathbf{1.228}$

*Beginning assets = $433,600 + $140,000 capital additions + Projected net operating profit of $130,632 = $704,232

ROI: $\dfrac{\text{Ending assets} - \text{Beginning assets}}{\text{Beginning assets}} = \dfrac{\text{Profit}}{\text{Beginning assets}} = \dfrac{\$130,632}{\$573,600} = \mathbf{22.8\%}$

Break-Even Level

$\dfrac{\text{Monthly contribution}}{\text{Monthly molds}} = \dfrac{\$16,286}{977} = \$16.67$ contribution per mold

$\dfrac{\text{Total monthly fixed cost}}{\text{Contribution per mold}} = \dfrac{\$5,400}{\$16.67} = 324$ molds to break even

$\dfrac{\text{Molds to break even}}{\text{Total molds made}} = \dfrac{324}{977} = 33.2\%$ molding capacity to break even

Measuring the Financial Impact of a Marketing Constraint

Before they went any further, Reuben wanted to see now what the financial consequence of the 300 wheel hub restriction would be, considering the benefits of the capital proposals. Jim said that would be simple to calculate. All they needed to do was run the algorithm and remove the single restriction on the number of wheel hubs.

Maximize $16.74(valve body) + $24.78(axle housing) +$10.12(differential case) + $18.35(wheel hub) +$19.10(brake caliper)

(Subject to the product routings and departmental capacities per Table 14.7.)

Table 14.12 Contribution Opportunity with Removing Marketing Constraint on Wheel Hubs

Product	Qty.	Department	Hrs. Required	Slack	Opportunity
Valve bodies	0	Core (existing)	194	31	0
Axle housings	170	Core (proposed)	78	102	0
Differential cases	0	Assembly	196	4	0
Wheel hubs	807	Molding	440	0	$38.40
Brake calipers	0	Cleaning (existing)	200	0	$10.72
		Cleaning (proposed)	0	150	0
		Grinding	181	19	0
Totals	**977**		**1,289**	**306**	
Maximum contribution possible $19,021					

Mr. Porter was surprised at what the optimized aggregate planning process could reveal: "In this case it is telling us that the wheel hub market constraint is valued at $32,820 per year ($19,021 per Table 14.12 – $16,286 per Table 14.9 = $2,735 × 12 = $32,820).

"In addition, our ROI could have been 28.5 percent [$19,021 × 12 = $228,252 – ($5,400 × 12) = $163,452 ÷ $573,600 = 28.5%] instead of the 22.8 percent that we are projecting. I would hate to think of what it would have cost us if I had insisted that we supply 50 brake calipers per month to my friend in North Carolina.

"Also, look how much simpler our projected product mix would have been, i.e., just axle housings and wheel hubs like we are accustomed to. Did you notice that without the market constraint we would not need to bring the old cleaning equipment in and have it reactivated? This is because there would be no differential cases in the marketing plan to process."

Table 14.12 confirms that the old cleaning equipment would have 150 hours of slack, and that was the total amount to be provided.

Mr. Porter continued: "I trust that you can all see just how sensitive our bottom line is to seemingly small operational and/or marketing fluctuations. The more important issue, however, is that now we have the ability to measure such activities.

"I hope you all noticed the tremendous synergy that is possible when we implement the requested capital projects simultaneously. The highest system ROI, when evaluating each project as if they were mutually exclusive, would have been attained with the addition of the molding machine with a 20.0 percent projected return. By implementing the three projects simultaneously, we could attain the 22.8 percent return.

"Well, now that we have the aggregate plan completed for our plant for next year, I've got a new challenge for us to consider. We have the opportunity to buy an existing facility similar to our plant. We will use optimization technology in the evaluation process. We will also apply the new concepts to the new proposed multiplant operation. This should be fun."

Summary—Key Points

These last chapters have clearly demonstrated that the marketing, operations, and capital plans represent integral parts of the seamless, integrative, and dynamic aggregate planning process.

This chapter has shown that:

- It is important to measure the financial impact of following nonstandard processes, of the need for replacement equipment, and of implementing capital proposals simultaneously.
- The capital portion of the planning process not only facilitates the achievement of the aggregate plan, but it also has a great deal to do with defining it.
- The anticipated marketing constraints have financial impacts important to the success of the plant.

SECTION VII

Evaluating Multiple Plant Operations Using Optimization Techniques

CHAPTER 15

Measuring the Real Financial Impact of Multiplant Operations

Up to this point we have illustrated the use of optimization technology in a single plant environment. Now we will illustrate these concepts in a multiple plant environment. With optimization technology, individual plant profit performance must be subsidiary to total corporate performance.

Chapter Contents

- Identifying potential merger candidates
- Separating the wheat from the chaff in the evaluation process
- Multiple plant operations should be evaluated as a single financial entity
- Individual plant performance must be subsidiary to total combined corporate performance
- Determining where improvements should be directed relative to the combined corporate operations
- Optimization techniques are required for total corporate management as well as in individual plant management
- Will the real constraints stand up please?
- A great presentation but with totally wrong content
- Proceeding on incorrect assumptions can have devastating results

Identifying Potential Merger Candidates

Mr. Porter had found a competitor, a branch of Crow-Bar Enterprises that had roughly the same capabilities and processes as their own plant. OpTek was interested initially because this prospective plant was active in the valve body and brake caliper markets, which would definitely complement OpTek's existing business. Crow-Bar also supplied one of OpTek's primary customers with a lesser amount of differential cases. Both plants had identical molding equipment and capacity.

Even though the manufacturing processes were roughly the same, there was some variation in variable costs. Selling prices were market determined, so they were the same as OpTek's. Crow-Bar also had the advantage of a lower monthly fixed cost than OpTek.

Crow-Bar's existing product mix and income statement follow:

Table 15.1 Crow-Bar's Existing Product Mix and Net Operating Profit

Crow Bar Manufacturing Variable Costing Income Statement					
Product	Qty.	Selling Price	Variable Cost	Contribution	Total Contribution
Valve bodies	220	$40.00	$23.50	$16.50	$3,630
Differential cases	75	30.00	21.00	9.00	675
Brake calipers	105	40.00	18.25	21.75	2,284
Totals	400				6,589
				Less monthly fixed cost	4,750
				Net operating profit	$1,839

OpTek's staff was impressed that this Crow-Bar plant was not using the traditional standard cost system. This was evidenced by the lack of allocated overhead on its income statement. OpTek also felt that there would be a significant opportunity for financial improvement inasmuch as Crow-Bar's product mix was not determined utilizing optimization technology or the OpTek Algorithm.

Separating the Wheat from the Chaff in the Evaluation Process

During the evaluation and negotiating process, Crow-Bar gave OpTek access to its routing files, cost files, and other manufacturing data as requested. In preparation for using the algorithm, Stephanie developed a routing matrix based on Crow-Bar's existing mix but also included proposed routings for the axle housing and wheel hub because Crow-Bar had the capability to make them also.

Table 15.2 Crow-Bar's Routing Matrix for Its Present Three Jobs Plus Proposed Routings for Axle Housings and Wheel Hubs

Department	Present Valve Body	**Proposed** Axle Housing	Present Differential Case	**Proposed** Wheel Hub	Present Brake Caliper	Capacity
Core .3	.8	.2	.4	.6	200 hrs.	
Assembly	.6	.3	.2	.3	.4	200 hrs.
Molding	.5	.5	.5	.5	.5	200 hrs.
Cleaning	.1	.8	.2	.2	.4	200 hrs.
Grinding	.2	.4	.2	.2	.6	200 hrs.

Now, OpTek didn't tell Crow-Bar, but it was about to determine Crow-Bar's profit potential using the OpTek Algorithm. OpTek wanted to make its decision on whether or not to buy Crow-Bar based on potential as well as present performance. Using Crow-Bar's calculated product contributions, Jim set up the objective:

Maximize **$16.50 (valve body) + $21.00 (axle housing) + $9.00(differential case) + $16.25(wheel hub) + $21.75(brake caliper)**

(Subject to product routings and departmental capacities per Table 15.2.) The resulting product mix and potential contribution are below.

Table 15.3 Crow-Bar's Proposed Product Mix and Maximum Contribution

Objective: **Maximize Contribution**

Product	Qty.	Department	Hrs. Required	Slack	Opportunity
Valve bodies	133	Core	200.00	0	$17.50
Axle housings	0	Assembly	186.67	13.33	0
Differential cases	0	Molding	200.00	0	22.50
Wheel hubs	0	Cleaning	120.00	80.00	0
Brake calipers	267	Grinding	186.67	13.33	0
Totals	400		893.34	106.66	
Maximum contribution possible $8,002					

The staff noted that the major change in the proposed product mix was the elimination of the differential cases and a different ratio of valve bodies to brake calipers. They also noted that the proposed contribution of $8,002 was more than their own of $7,800. This fact, combined with Crow-Bar's lower monthly fixed cost, would give Crow-Bar monthly net operating profit of $3,252 versus OpTek's net operating profit of $2,800.

The next step was to consolidate the data sets so as to preview what the combined operation would look like. The objective included the consideration of all ten parts with their respective contributions:

Maximize *OpTek's* $15.00(valve body) + $22.50(axle housing) + $10.00(differential case) + $17.50(wheel hub) + $19.00(brake caliper) + *Crow-bar's* $16.50 (valve body) + $21.00 (axle housing) + $9.00(differential case) + $16.25(wheel hub) + $21.75(brake caliper)

(Subject to product routings and departmental capacities in Tables 2.4 [p. 16] and 15.2.)

Jim commented that it was important to make sure that the correct part contributions followed their respective routings, i.e., OpTek's original five parts were routed through OpTek's facility (Table 2.4) while the latter five parts were routed through Crow-Bar's facility (Table 15.2).

Table 15.4 Contribution Maximizing Product Mix for Combined Operation

Objective: **Maximize Contribution**					
Product	Qty.	Department	Hrs. Required	Slack	Opportunity
Valve bodies (O)	0	Core (O)	200.00	0	$10.00
Axle housings (O)	160	Assembly (O)	80.00	120.00	0
Differential cases (O)	0	Molding (O)	200.00	0	29.00
Wheel hubs (O)	240	Cleaning (O)	136.00	64.00	0
Brake calipers (O)	0	Grinding (O)	96.00	104.00	0
Valve bodies (CB)	133	Core (CB)	200.00	0	17.50
Axle housings (CB)	0	Assembly (CB)	186.67	13.33	0
Differential cases (CB)	0	Molding (CB)	200.00	0	22.50
Wheel hubs (CB)	0	Cleaning (CB)	120.00	80.00	0
Brake calipers (CB)	267	Grinding (CB)	186.67	13.33	0
Totals	800		1,605.34	394.66	
Maximum contribution possible $15,802					

Products and departments are differentiated by **(O)** for OpTek and **(CB)** for Crow-Bar. The combined contribution of $15,802 confirms that the data set is complete and correct.

Multiple Plant Operations Should Be Evaluated As a Single Financial Entity

At this point, the evaluation really got serious. OpTek's staff had to accept the premise that not only was individual department performance not critical, but also that *individual plant performance must be subsidiary to total corporate performance.*

Of course, after learning how to manage OpTek, Mr. Porter quickly inquired about the potential synergy involved with a merger. They were about to find out. First, however, Jim made several points about the combined operation in Table 15.4:

1. Both plants are constrained by their respective core and molding departments.
2. Although the processes are similar, the production rates vary between plants. The molding processes, however, are exactly the same.

Upon hearing these points, Mr. Porter asked about the potential benefits of combining the molding operations into one work center with 400 hours available instead of two individual work centers with 200 hours each.

Jim concealed a snicker as he politely explained that 200 hours in one plant plus 200 hours in the other plant totaled 400 hours no matter how you cut it. He asked what difference it would make if there was one molding center with 400 available hours or two plants with 200 available hours each?

Mr. Porter told them to humor him and run the scenario through the OpTek Algorithm.

So Jim set up the objective to maximize contribution. He set up a *single molding center with a capacity of 400 hours.* With the exception of molding, the plants would run as separate entities. The five original OpTek parts would be routed through the existing OpTek plant, except for molding, which would be combined. The proposed five Crow-Bar parts would be routed through the existing Crow-Bar plant, again except for the combined molding operation:

> Maximize $15.00(valve body) + $22.50(axle housing) + $10.00(differential case) + $17.50(wheel hub) + $19.00(brake caliper) + $16.50(valve body) + $21.00(axle housing) + $9.00(differential case) + $16.25(wheel hub) + $21.75(brake caliper)

(Subject to product routings and departmental capacities per Tables 2.4 and 15.2, with the exception of molding, with a single capacity of 400 hours.)

Table 15.5 Contribution Possible with Combined Molding Capacity of 400 Hours

Objective: **Maximize Contribution**					
Product	**Qty.**	**Department**	**Hrs. Required**	**Slack**	**Opportunity**
Valve bodies (O)	0	Core (O)	200.00	0	$10.00
Axle housings (O)	120	Assembly (O)	93.33	106.67	0
Differential cases (O)	0	**Molding (combined)**	400.00	0	29.00
Wheel hubs (O)	347	Cleaning (O)	118.67	81.33	0
Brake calipers (O)	0	Grinding (O)	105.33	94.67	0
Valve bodies (CB)	0	Core (CB)	200.00	0	12.08
Axle housings (CB)	0	Assembly (CB)	132.33	67.67	0
Differential cases (CB)	0	Cleaning (CB)	132.33	67.67	0
Wheel hubs (CB)	0	Grinding (CB)	200.00	0	7.29
Brake calipers (CB)	333				
Totals	**800**		**1,581.99**	**418.01**	
Maximum contribution possible $16,017					

The others just waited for Mr. Porter to explain the results: "You see, when each plant has a molding machine with a capacity of 200 hours, or 400 molds, each plant's output is limited to 400 total molds or parts. But when you combine the molding process into a single work center, one plant's output can exceed 400 molds. In reality, we would leave the molding units in each plant, but instead of there being two work centers with 400 molds capacity each, we would consider just one molding center with capacity of 800 molds. I think you can see how it works. One of the molding machines could make some molds for the other plant."

He continued, "The present OpTek plant per Table 15.5 could now produce 467 parts—120 axle housings + 347 wheel hubs—while the Crow-Bar plant could produce and ship just 333 brake calipers. The molding unit at the Crow-Bar plant would make 67 molds for the OpTek plant. There is, in fact, some synergism already evident."

Stephanie then pointed out that while *combined contribution increased* from $15,802 to $16,017, the *combined utilization decreased* from 80.3 percent to 79.1 percent.

Individual Plant Performance Must Be Subsidiary to Total Combined Corporate Performance

Now the Crow-Bar plant could charge OpTek anything they wished for the 67 molds, but the combined enterprise contribution would remain at $16,017. *Individual plant performance would not be as important as adherence to the combined production plan.*

Jim noted that combining the two molding units into a single work center changed the relative performance of each plant. Before the molding consolidation the OpTek plant contributed $7,800 per month and the Crow-ar plant contributed $8,002. Now the OpTek plant would contribute $8,772, while the Crow-Bar plant would generate $7,243 in contribution.

Table 15.6 Proposed Relative Contribution From Each Plant

OpTek Plant			
Product	**Qty.**	**Contribution Each**	**Plant Contribution**
Axle housings	120	$22.50	$2,700
Wheel hubs	347	17.50	6,072
	467		**$8,772**
Crow-Bar Plant			
Product	**Qty.**	**Contribution Each**	**Plant Contribution**
Brake calipers	333	$21.75	$7,243
Total combined net operating profit = $6,265 ($8,772 + $7,243) – ($5,000 + $4,750).			

Mr. Porter commented that this was a good example of how *total corporate performance must supercede individual plant performance.* If this transaction goes through, they would need to change their performance measures: "I believe that adherence to production plans will be the primary indicator."

Determining Where Improvements Should Be Directed Relative to the Combined Corporate Operations

He continued: "If we can buy this plant for what I think we can, we will have $100,000 capital remaining and available for work center expansion. The three of you will please advise me how best to invest this money. The criteria will be the increase in operating cash flow."

Stephanie went to work and gathered vendor bids for capital equipment. They met, without Mr. Porter, and reviewed the bids. They wanted to prepare a recommendation package to present to Mr. Porter, complete with proposed capital budget and estimated cash flow information.

Table 15.7 Capital Equipment Cost for Each Work Center

Equipment	Cost
Core machine	$ 25,000
Assembly machine	15,000
Molding machine	100,000
Cleaning machine	20,000
Grinding machine	10,000

Their choices were numerous. They joked that they could buy four core machines or five cleaning machines. Or they could buy six assembly stations and one grinding machine, or they could buy just one molding machine.

Optimization Techniques Are Required for Total Corporate Management As Well As in Individual Plant Management

They knew that any work center expansion must begin by examining the constrained work centers in Table 15.5.

Upon examination, they noted that there were several constrained work centers, i.e., core departments in both plants, the combined molding operation, and the grinding department in Crow-Bar's plant. Their initial thought was that any benefit from investing the entire capital budget in a new molding machine would be minimal inasmuch as both plants had constrained core departments. Besides, they reasoned, we could add core machines to both plants and still have $50,000 left. So they simulated adding core capacity to both plants. The objective was contribution maximization:

Maximize $15.00(valve body) + $22.50(axle housing) + $10.00(differential case) + $17.50(wheel hub) + $19.00(brake caliper) + $16.50(valve body) + $21.00(axle housing) + $9.00(differential case) + $16.25(wheel hub) + $21.75(brake caliper)

(Subject to product routings and departmental capacities per Tables 2.4 and 15.2.)

The only change to the data set is that each core work center will have a capacity of 400 hours instead of 200 hours.

Table 15.8 Proposed Contribution When Core Capacity Is Added to Both Plants

Objective: **Maximize Contribution**					
Product	Qty.	Department	Hrs. Required	Slack	Opportunity
Valve bodies (O)	0	Core (O)	258.75	141.25	0
Axle housings (O)	263	Assembly (O)	85.00	115.00	0
Differential cases (O)	0	Molding (combined)	400.00	0	$33.33
Wheel hubs (O)	162	Cleaning (O)	200.00	0	8.33
Brake calipers (O)	0	Grinding (O)	110.75	88.75	0
Valve bodies (CB)	0	Core (CB)	250.00	150.00	0
Axle housings (CB)	125	Assembly (CB)	137.50	62.50	0
Differential cases (CB)	0	Cleaning (CB)	200.00	0	1.77
Wheel hubs (CB)	0	Grinding (CB)	200.00	0	7.29
Brake calipers (CB)	250		1,842.50	557.50	
Totals	800				
Maximum contribution possible $16,815					

They all noted numerous changes in this proposed scenario:

1. Total enterprise utilization has decreased from 79.1 percent to 76.8 percent. Remember that with the addition of core capacity in both plants, the available hours were 2,400 (1,842.50 ÷ 2,400 = 76.8%).

2. The new core machines in both plants were, in their viewpoint, very much underutilized. The core machine in the OpTek plant would experience utilization of just 29.4 percent (hours used = 200 – 141.25 = 58.75 ÷ 200 = 29.4%). The core machine in the Crow-Bar plant would have a 25 percent utilization (hours used = 200 – 150 = 50 ÷ 200 = 25%).

3. They reasoned that the relatively poor utilization of the core machines was attributable to the remaining downstream constraints, i.e., both cleaning departments and Crow-Bar's grinding department.

4. The answer, they thought, would be in removing the remaining constraints other than molding, which would require their total available capital funds. Jim checked the balance of the capital funds to ensure that there would be enough left to add capacity to the two cleaning departments and Crow-Bar's grinding department.

Department	Cost per Machine	Number Required	Capital Required
Cleaning	$20,000	2	$40,000
Grinding	10,000	1	10,000
		Total	$50,000

They confirmed that they had sufficient funds to remove all remaining constraints except molding. So they activated the OpTek Algorithm with the contribution maximization objective. The data set was modified to add capacity to both cleaning departments as well to Crow-Bar's grinding department. Below is a summary of the departmental capacities included in the data set.

Table 15.9 Combined Capacity with All Constraints Removed Except Molding

Company and Department	Capacity in Hours
OpTek Core	400
OpTek Assembly	200
OpTek Cleaning	400
OpTek Grinding	200
Combined Molding	400
Crow-Bar Core	400
Crow-Bar Assembly	200
Crow-Bar Cleaning	400
Crow-Bar Grinding	400
Total	3,000

They were all elated with the following results of the algorithm (Table 15.10 and 15.11).

1. Contribution had improved by another 5.7 percent, from $16,815 to $17,775.
2. Enterprise utilization had decreased from 76.8 percent to 66.6 percent.
3. The resulting product mix was a marketer's dream, i.e., just axle housings and brake calipers.
4. The resulting product mix was also a manufacturer's dream. The existing OpTek plant could concentrate on axle housings while the Crow-Bar facility could concentrate on brake calipers and make 100 molds for OpTek.
5. Jim was interested in the fact that the existing OpTek plant would contribute over 63 percent of total contribution to the combined enterprise.

Table 15.10 Proposed Enterprise Product Mix and Contribution When All Production Constraints Are Removed Except Molding

Objective: **Maximize Contribution**					
Product	**Qty.**	**Department**	**Hrs. Required**	**Slack**	**Opportunity**
Valve bodies (O)	0	**Core (O)**	400	0	$ .94
Axle housings (O)	500	Assembly (O)	100	100	0
Differential cases (O)	0	Molding (combined)	400	0	43.50
Wheel hubs (O)	0	**Cleaning (O)**	350	50	0
Brake calipers (O)	0	Grinding (O)	150	50	0
Valve bodies (CB)	0	**Core (CB)**	180	220	0
Axle housings (CB)	0	Assembly (CB)	120	80	0
Differential cases (CB)	0	Cleaning (CB)	120	280	0
Wheel hubs (CB)	0	**Grinding (CB)**	180	220	0
Brake calipers (CB)	300				
Totals	**800**		**2,000**	**1,000**	
Maximum contribution possible $17,775					

Table 15.11 Proposed Contribution by Plant

OpTek Contribution		
Axle housing = 500 × $22.50 = $11,250	63.29%	
Crow-Bar Contribution		
Brake caliper = 300 × $21.75 = $ 6,525	36.71%	
Totals	**$17,775**	**100.00%**

They were all very enthusiastic as they worked together to prepare the report for Mr. Porter.

Will the Real Constraints Stand Up Please?

Then out of the blue Stephanie said: "There has got to be something wrong here. According to Table 15.10 there are three departments with idle capacity (slack) of more than 200 hours. We added capacity in 200 hour blocks."

As they reasoned together, Jim commented, "I really don't understand this. Before we simulated the addition of capacity to both cleaning departments and Crow-Bar's grinding department in Table 15.10, those three departments were the only remaining constraints except molding. Let's take another look at Table 15.8 to confirm this." Sure enough, Table 15.8 confirmed their thinking.

So they decided to try going back to where they began, i.e., after they combined the molding units into a single work center per Mr. Porter's suggestion. That scenario was documented in Table 15.5 (p. 166).

Now they really had to concentrate. They knew from the end results in Table 15.10, that they really didn't need to add capacity to those work centers that now have in excess of 200 hours slack. They also knew that capacity was needed in OpTek's cleaning department per Table 15.8 (p. 169). This was confirmed in Table 15.10, which shows only 50 hours of slack after adding 200 hours capacity. The interesting fact is that OpTek's cleaning department was not originally constrained in Table 15.5, so they didn't initially add capacity there. That department didn't surface as a constraint until after they added capacity to both core departments.

"Let's suppose that we started the planning for our expansion in Table 15.5. Could we get the same end result as Table 15.10, i.e., a $17,775 contribution if we added only another core machine and cleaning machine to the original OpTek plant? That does appear to be the case. We really won't know until we try it."

So they activated the algorithm once again with contribution maximization as the objective. They listed the departmental capacities in the data set as follows:

Table 15.12 Enterprise Capacity After Adding Equipment Only to OpTek's Core and Cleaning Departments

Plant and Department	Available Hours
OpTek Core	400
OpTek Assembly	200
OpTek Cleaning	400
OpTek Grinding	200
Combined Molding	400
Crow-Bar Core	200
Crow-Bar Assembly	200
Crow-Bar Cleaning	200
Crow-Bar Grinding	200
Total	2,400

They ran the algorithm with the following results:

Table 15.13 Combined Facility Contribution When Adding Only Core and Cleaning Capacity to Original OpTek Plant

Objective: **Maximize Contribution**					
Product	**Qty.**	**Department**	**Hrs. Required**	**Slack**	**Opportunity**
Valve bodies (O)	0	Core (O)	400	0	$ .94
Axle housings (O)	500	Assembly (O)	100	100	0
Differential cases (O)	0	Molding (combined)	400	0	43.50
Wheel hubs (O)	0	Cleaning (O)	350	50	0
Brake calipers (O)	0	Grinding (O)	150	50	0
Valve bodies (CB)	0	Core (CB)	180	20	0
Axle housings (CB)	0	Assembly (CB)	120	80	0
Differential cases (CB)	0	Cleaning (CB)	120	80	0
Wheel hubs (CB)	0	Grinding (CB)	180	20	0
Brake calipers (CB)	300				
Totals	**800**		**2,000**	**400**	
Maximum contribution possible $17,775					

They realized that their thinking was sound. So they asked to make the presentation to Mr. Porter about the benefits of buying the Crow-Bar plant.

A Great Presentation but with Totally Wrong Content

As the meeting began, Jim did most of the talking: "Based on our past experience with the OpTek Algorithm, we were able to intuitively examine the results after you suggested combining the molding operations and arrive at a very quick recommendation."

Upon hearing Jim's claim, both Stephanie and Reuben just grinned in silence.

"We can generate a combined enterprise contribution of $17,775 per month. In addition, we can accomplish this with only $45,000 capital investment and have $55,000 left over. The combined operation will have an overall utilization of 83.33 percent, which we think is excellent. The proposed product mix will be very marketing and manufacturing friendly, with only axle housings being produced in the existing OpTek plant and brake calipers in the Crow-Bar plant. The existing OpTek plant will contribute 63 percent of combined contribution, while the Crow-Bar plant will contribute the remaining 37 percent."

Jim referred them to Table 15.11. "We suggest that we proceed with the purchase of the Crow-Bar plant."

Proceeding on Incorrect Assumptions Can Have Devastating Results

Mr. Porter agreed with their final suggestion to proceed with the purchase of the Crow-Bar plant: "I might recommend several minor changes, however, to your overall recommendation. Jim, take the entire $100,000 available capital and buy another molding machine and have it installed in our present OpTek facility. At the same time go to the bank and borrow $25,000 for an additional core machine and install that also in our existing facility. Forget about any additions to the Crow-Bar plant."

Then he got up and returned to his office. They looked at each other thinking: How in the world could he make such a rash recommendation when we're the ones that have been doing all the analyses?

Stephanie said they'd better at least try his recommendation, so they went back to Table 15.5. To this table they simulated the addition of another molding machine, which provided another 200 hours for a total molding capacity of 600 hours, or 1,200 molds. They wanted to check the boss's recommendation in steps so they tested only molding initially. They activated the algorithm with contribution maximization as the objective and obtained the following results:

Table 15.14 Potential Contribution with Adding Just One Molding Machine, Bringing Total Molding Capacity to 1,200 Molds

Objective: **Maximize Contribution**					
Product	**Qty.**	**Department**	**Hrs. Required**	**Slack**	**Opportunity**
Valve bodies (O)	0	Core (O)	200.00	0	$37.50
Axle housings (O)	0	Assembly (O)	139.17	60.83	0
Differential cases (O)	175	**Molding (combined)**	**600.00**	0	12.50
Wheel hubs (O)	608	Cleaning (O)	95.83	104.17	0
Brake calipers (O)	0	Grinding (O)	139.17	60.83	0
Valve bodies (CB)	167	Core (CB)	200.00	0	21.67
Axle housings (CB)	0	Assembly (CB)	200.00	0	6.25
Differential cases (CB)	0	Cleaning (CB)	116.67	83.33	0
Wheel hubs (CB)	0	Grinding (CB)	183.33	16.67	0
Brake calipers (CB)	250				
Totals	**1,200**		**1,874.17**	**325.83**	
Maximum contribution possible $20,583					

Jim exclaimed: "Maybe he was right. Look at that amount of contribution. The opportunity really shot up also in the core department in our existing plant. Let's go ahead and show the addition of a new core machine along with the new molding machine and rerun the algorithm."

Table 15.15 Potential Contribution When Adding One Core Machine and One Molding Machine to the Original OpTek Plant

Objective: **Maximize Contribution**					
Product	Qty.	Department	Hrs. Required	Slack	Opportunity
Valve bodies (O)	0	Core (O)	345.44	45.56	0
Axle housings (O)	190	Assembly (O)	173.33	26.67	0
Differential cases (O)	0	Molding (combined)	600.00	0	$33.33
Wheel hubs (O)	677	Cleaning (O)	200.00	0	8.33
Brake calipers (O)	0	Grinding (O)	192.22	7.78	0
Valve bodies (CB)	0	Core (CB)	200.00	0	8.47
Axle housings (CB)	0	Assembly (CB)	133.33	66.67	0
Differential cases (CB)	0	Cleaning (CB)	133.33	66.67	0
Wheel hubs (CB)	0	Grinding (CB)	200.00	0	?
Brake calipers (CB)	333				
Totals	1,200		2,186.65	213.35	
Maximum contribution possible $23,365					

They were pretty humbled by what they saw:

1. Contribution had increased by 45.8 percent from $16,017 in Table 15.5 to $23,365 in Table 15.15 ($23,365– $16,017 = $7,348 × 12 = $88,176).
2. Even though they realized that total facility utilization was not a focal point, they did notice that utilization improved from 79.2 percent in Table 15.5 to 91.1 percent per Table 15.15.
3. They noted that the Crow-Bar plant would still be used to produce just 333 brake calipers plus make 67 molds for the OpTek plant. The OpTek plant could still concentrate on axle housings and wheel hubs.
4. The incremental contribution of $88,176 per year would make short work of the $125,000 capital investment required to achieve it.
5. When they originally looked at the Crow-Bar plant it would contribute more than half of the combined contribution, i.e., $8,002 of the combined

total of $15,802. Now the original OpTek plant would contribute 69 percent of the combined contribution:

Original OpTek Plant
Axle housings 190 × $22.50 =$ 4,275
Wheel hubs 677 × $17.50 =$11,848

$16,123 = 69%

Original Crow-Bar Plant
Brake calipers 333 × $21.75 $ 7,242 =   31%

Combined Enterprise   **$23,365 = 100%**

Jim remarked that Mr. Porter was right again: "We should have never assumed that investing the entire $100,000 in a new molding machine would be the incorrect action. I remember that we came to that conclusion because both plants were constrained by their core departments. Once again, our flawed logic gives way to the results of optimization technology.

"He sure was right. We can tell that he's spent a lot of time with his PC playing with the OpTek Algorithm," voiced the others.

They all realized one more time why Mr. Porter was general manager.

Summary—Key Points

Perhaps the major lesson to be learned from this chapter is that:
- Preconceived results or intuition will really foul up an optimization opportunity.
- Remember, if we choose to use optimization technology, we cannot include any other factors without seriously diluting the results.

Also to be learned from this chapter is:

- A plant must be on the lookout for, be able to recognize, and know how to successfully evaluate potential merger candidates.
- The maximum financial performance for a multiple plant operation will occur only if all operating units are evaluated as a single combined financial entity.
- Traditional wisdom may tell us to have separate plants compete with each other relative to individual plant performance. That may satisfy existing performance criteria, but that action will certainly lead to suboptimal performance at the corporate level.

SECTION VIII

Summary—Retracing the Steps to Becoming a User of Optimization Techniques

CHAPTER 16

Summarizing OpTek's Journey from Traditional Practices to Optimization Techniques

This closing chapter summarizes the journey that OpTek took away from the seven deadly sins of manufacturing and into the realm of optimization technology. It also addresses the learning process encountered by the staff as they learned how to use and apply optimization techniques.

Chapter Contents

- Stephanie has learned a great deal about financial issues
- Jim has learned a great deal about plant operations
- Reuben has learned a great deal about plant operations too
- Jim compares the benefits resulting from optimization technology with the limitations of the old standard cost system
- Reuben describes the benefits available to the marketing function by being able to define their own niche
- A new incentive for the marketing people
- Stephanie and Jim summarize their findings relative to optimization technology in the capital budgeting process
- Stephanie summarizes the importance of focused process improvements
- Mr. Porter announces their attainment of being classified as a user of optimization technology
- Interdisciplinary teaming was required in order to achieve their accomplishments

After the dust had settled relative to the acquisition of Crow-Bar, Mr. Porter called his staff together to announce that, in his opinion, they had learned to manage their operations with optimization technology. He asked them to prepare a list of things that they had learned during the recent months on their journey.

Stephanie Has Learned a Great Deal About Financial Measures

"With a given set of equipment, available products, and their respective routings, we discovered that there is one optimum product mix that will maximize our operating profit. I believe it is appropriate to express our capacity in terms of contribution dollars instead of the traditional units."

Jim Has Learned a Great Deal About Plant Operations

"We should consider the $7,800 contribution from our profit maximizing product mix to be our opportunity/capacity and determine our level of effectiveness based on that benchmark.

"For example, if we must, or think that it is politically expedient, to make something not included in our optimum product mix, we should be aware of the cost to do it. If we choose to make a mix that results in, say, $7,200 in contribution per month, then we could say we operated at 92.3 percent capacity ($7,200 ÷ $7,800 = 92.3%) even though we made 400 molds."

Reuben Has Learned a Great Deal About Plant Operations Too

"A lesson that we learned is that just because we have a state-of-the-art production process doesn't mean that we can make all parts better than our competition. From now on we'll always be open to subcontracting."

Jim Compares the Benefits Resulting from Optimization Technology with the Limitations of the Old Standard Cost System

"We had relied on our standard cost system for years, not only to measure performance but also to make product decisions. This experience was really an eye opener. The major thing we learned was that if an action doesn't have a positive effect on total contribution, then we should rethink that action. Let me summarize several limitations of planning and controlling with a standard cost system:

1. Standard costing assumes that all manufacturing costs, fixed and variable, can be assigned to individual products via an appropriate cost driver.
2. Standard costing results in variance chasing. *When using standard costing as a performance measure, the only way to affect profit is by cost reduction.* The product mix is not considered to be a key issue because all products have a margin assigned over and above total product standard costs. Variances accrue to departments that assume that costs are assignable and controllable by managers. *Variance chasing may promote dysfunctional behavior.*
3. Standard costing causes micro-management of all work centers. Work centers are evaluated on their localized performance primarily relating to budget variances and utilization. Now we let the work center utilization be determined, or pulled, by the requirements of the optimum product mix.
4. Relying on standard costing may lead to suboptimal decisions:
   - Standard cost information pointed to the production of 400 wheel hubs as the best product mix to maximize profit because it had the highest gross profit of any available product.
   - Standard cost information indicated that we should not outsource any axle housings or wheel hubs because our total standard costs for these products were less than the "buy" price.
   - Standard costing implies that we can make all parts equally well. If we apply a constant markup percentage, the reasoning is that all parts are equally desirable relative to profitability.
   - We also learned that while activity-based costing may result in the most accurate product standard costs, we found no direct relationship between standard cost accuracy and operating profit enhancement."

Reuben Describes the Benefits Available to Their Marketing Function by Being Able to Define Their Own Niche

"I certainly see an increased role for the operations people in defining where our marketing efforts should be focused. I didn't realize what an advantage it was to know what we do best. It's like defining our own niche. No more choosing products according to gross profit or percent markup over total standard cost."

A New Incentive for the Marketing People

"By the way, perhaps my incentive plan should be based on percent effectiveness relative to our contribution opportunity. The old way based on total sales is not relevant because our product mix doesn't necessarily relate to total sales volume."

Stephanie and Jim Summarize Their Findings Relative to Optimization Technology in the Capital Budgeting Process

Stephanie began, "Now the capital budgeting process is entirely different. Instead of limiting the savings to labor and overhead relative to the existing product mix, we let the OpTek Algorithm define the new optimum product mix made possible with the proposed process improvements or capacity additions."

Jim added, "The contribution reflected with the new optimum product mix, less the contribution achieved with existing conditions/processes, is the incremental cash flow provided by the proposal."

Stephanie continued, "We also learned very quickly to limit our capital proposals to constrained work centers. To increase capacity or efficiency in a non-constrained work center proved to be foolish."

Jim said, "The three basic lessons that we learned about capital proposal justification can be summarized as follows:

1. The relevant cash flow should be determined by comparing the facility contribution provided with the proposal to what it was without the proposal.
2. The actual ranking of financial desirability of the alternatives (after cash flows are determined by using the OpTek Algorithm) should be based on total system ROI and not on individual project IRR (internal rate of return).
3. The constrained work centers that surface or exist when the contribution maximizing product mix is run should define the area where future capital funds should be directed."

Stephanie Summarizes the Importance of Focused Process Improvements

"We were also myopic concerning manufacturing process improvements. We learned not to expend time and other resources on processes associated with non-

---

constrained work centers. They already have slack, or idle time. There is no virtue in increasing idle time."

Mr. Porter Announces Their Attainment of Being Classified as a User of Optimization Technology

"I'm very impressed with not only what you have learned but also your depth of understanding of it. We can make the products and do it better than ever before. Product and process technology was not our problem. Our greatest challenge was to learn how to identify and then focus our efforts on eliminating the waste associated with the seven deadly sins of manufacturing. We as manufacturers need to increase our skills in recognizing which operational activities are relative to profit improvement and which are not."

Interdisciplinary Teaming Was Required in Order to Achieve Their Accomplishments

Mr. Porter continued, "I was particularly impressed by how you worked as a team. Jim, it used to be that the others were intimidated with the financial aspect of our business. That is no longer the case. Inasmuch as everything we have and do in our plant begins with cash and will return to cash, it is imperative that we are all intimately knowledgeable with the financial aspects of our business.

"Jim, I'm also pleased that you finally got over the overhead absorption question. It took quite awhile for you to see the futility of such a practice. I'm also glad that you discovered the inherent limitations of activity-based accounting.

"Stephanie, in your case I'm pleased that you finally got over the utilization question. It was interesting to watch your expression as profitability increased when overall facility utilization decreased."

"Reuben, I was glad that you came to the realization that the operations aspect of our business has so much validity. It was good to hear you comment that the manufacturing people should have a bigger say in where the marketing efforts should be focused.

"Now that our priorities are in proper order we can once again concentrate on some of our execution related challenges. And now that we have identified and eliminated the seven deadly sins of manufacturing and we know what our optimum product mix is, let's see that our manufacturing process is synchronized and the right work once again flows smoothly and timely through the plant. Good job all of you!"

Summary

This summary chapter highlighted the following key points:

- A great amount of interaction between marketing, finance, and operations is needed for success in this new way of managing.
- Basic changes and adjustments in thinking are required to adopt optimization technology.
- Each of the major functions needs to become acutely aware of one other and the effects of their interaction on plant operation.
- The financial impact of a plant's operating activities can be measured only at the total plant contribution level.
- There are tremendous benefits from using optimization techniques as compared to the limitations of the old standard cost system.
- Optimization techniques bring improvement in the capital budgeting process.
- Focused process improvements are important for ongoing success.

    When a plant has a grasp of the application of optimization techniques, it:

- Can choose feasible manufacturing strategies.
- Has the ability to choose the best strategic alternatives, i.e., those actions which will generate the highest level of profit possible.
- Is able to define its own niche in the market, providing new incentives for the marketing department.
- Can see that the best first step for everyone wishing to take the optimization journey is to eliminate several terms from their vocabulary, starting with *overhead absorption*, *idle capacity variance*, *fixed cost per unit*, and *gross profit*.

SECTION IX

Appendices

Activity-Based Costing: Determination of ABC Rates Presented in Chapter 2

OpTek Corporation incurs $5,000 per month of fixed costs—costs that are a function of time and not related to the level of production activity.

If any part of this $5,000 were unit driven, it wouldn't appear in the overhead pool to begin with. That part would bypass the assignment process and be directly traced to the ultimate cost object, which in the present case are individual products.

Activity-based costing recognizes the existence of necessary manufacturing costs that are not unit driven. Such costs are caused by "doing something" to enhance the production process and are termed activities. Such costs:

1. Are necessary to accomplish the production process.
2. Cannot be traced directly to specific units of production.
3. May benefit a specific batch, or a given product line, or the facility as a whole.

Consider Table A.1. The first item of cost listed in Table A.1 is equipment lease in the amount of $400. Let's say that the equipment is HVAC equipment that benefits the entire facility. Logic would suggest that this $400 per month be assigned to molds inasmuch as each mold benefits from HVAC equipment regardless of the product contained in the mold. If molding is OpTek's predominant production constraint, with a capacity of 400 molds each month, then each mold would be assigned $1.00 for the HVAC equipment lease.

The next two items of overhead cost in Table A.1 are product engineering and quality checks. These two activities can be identified by and associated with

Table A.1 OpTek's $5,000 Monthly Fixed Overhead Identified as to the Level of Production That Benefits from the Given Activities

Description	Amount	Driver Level
Equipment lease	$ 400	Facility
Product engineering	$1,000	Product line
Quality checks	$1,500	Product line
Material handling	$1,500	Batch
Setups	$ 600	Batch
Total	**$5,000**	
Facility-driven pool	$ 400	
Product line-driven pool	$2,500	
Batch-driven pool	$2,100	
Total	**$5,000**	

given product lines. Table A.2 defines the specific activity-based driver, the cost of this activity per month, the capacity of each driver per month, and the resultant cost per each activity occurrence.

Table A.2 Determination of Cost Per Each Activity Classified as Product-Line Drivers

Product-Line Drivers
1. Product Engineering: $1,000 per month Activity-based driver = Engineering changes Capacity of engineering changes = 10 per month Cost of product engineering assigned per engineering change = $100
2. Quality Checks: $1,500 per Month Activity-based driver = Number of ultrasonic tests Capacity of ultrasonic tests = 20 per month Cost of quality checks assigned per ultrasonic test = $75

The last two items of cost in Table A.1 are material handling and setups. These final two activities can be identified and associated with specific batches of product per Table A.3.

The next step is to assign the costs associated with the product-line drivers to each product based on the product mix of 80 of each part. (For ease of understanding, we will consider that each category of fixed cost is totally assigned to the product mix and, subsequently, that there will not be any unassigned fixed overhead variance to explain.)

Table A.3 Determination of Cost of Each Activity Classified as Batch-Level Drivers

Batch-Level Drivers
1. Material Handling: $1,500 per month 　Activity-based driver = Material movements 　Material movements required per month = 60 　Cost of material handling assigned per material movement = $25
2. Setup: $600 　Activity-based driver = Machine setups 　Setups required per month = 60 　Cost of setups assigned per setup = $10

Table A.4 Determination of Each Product's Unit Fixed Cost Attributable to Product-Line Cost Drivers

Assignment of Product Engineering Costs				
(1) Product	(2) Number of Engineering Change Orders	(3) Cost per Change Order	(4) Product Engineering Cost Assigned	(5) Unit Cost for Product Engineering
Valve body	3	$100	$ 300	$ 3.75
Axle housing	4	$100	$ 400	$ 5.00
Differential case	0	$100	0	0
Wheel hub	1	$100	$ 100	$ 1.25
Brake caliper	2	$100	$ 200	$ 2.50
			Total $1,000	
Assignment of Quality Checks Costs				
(6) Product	(7) Number of Ultrasonic Tests	(8) Cost per Ultrasonic Test	(9) Quality Checks Cost Assigned	(10) Unit Cost for Quality Checks
Valve body	4	$75	$ 300	$3.75
Axle housing	2	$75	$ 150	$1.875
Differential case	2	$75	$ 150	$1.875
Wheel hub	7	$75	$ 525	$6.56
Brake caliper	5	$75	$ 375	$4.69
			Total $1,500	

Column explanation for Table A.4:

(1) Product identity
(2) Activity-based driver for product engineering and estimated number of engineering change orders that each product is expected to incur each month
(3) Cost per engineering change order from Table A.2
(4) Column 2 × column 3 = column 4
(5) Column 4 ÷ 80 of each part = column 5
(6) Product identity
(7) Activity-based driver for quality checks and estimated number of ultrasonic tests that each product will require each month
(8) Cost per ultrasonic test from Table A.2
(9) Column 7 × column 8 = column 9
(10) Column 9 ÷ 80 of each part = column 10

Now we can determine the product unit fixed cost that is attributable to product-line drivers.

Table A.5 Determination of Unit Fixed Cost Assigned to Each Product Caused by Product-Line Drivers

Product	(a) Unit Cost for Engineering Changes	(b) Unit Cost for Ultrasonic Tests	(c) Unit Cost of Product-Line Drivers (a) + (b)
Valve body	$3.75	$3.75	$7.50
Axle housing	$5.00	$1.875	$6.875
Differential case	$ 0	$1.875	$1.875
Wheel hub	$1.25	$6.56	$7.81
Brake caliper	$2.50	$4.69	$7.19

Now we can analyze the two items of cost identified as batch-level drivers and determine the resulting product unit cost associated with the material handling and setup activities.

Table A.6 Determination of Unit Fixed Cost Assigned to Each Product Caused by Batch-Level Drivers

			Assignment of Material Handling Costs		
(1)	**(2)**	**(3)**	**(4)**	**(5)**	**(6)**
Product	Batch Size	Batches per Month	Cost per Batch	Cost per Month	Unit Cost for Material Handling
Valve body	20	4	$25	$ 100	$1.25
Axle housing	4	20	$25	$ 500	$6.25
Differential case	5	16	$25	$ 400	$5.00
Wheel hub	8	10	$25	$ 250	$3.125
Brake caliper	8	10	$25	$ 250	$3.125
				Total $1,500	

		Assignment of Setup Costs		
(7)	**(8)**	**(9)**	**(10)**	**(11)**
Product	Batches per Month	Cost per Setup	Setup Cost	Unit Cost for Setup
Valve body	4	$10	$ 40	$ .50
Axle housing	20	$10	$200	$2.50
Differential case	16	$10	$160	$2.00
Wheel hub	10	$10	$100	$1.25
Brake caliper	10	$10	$100	$1.25
			Total $600	

Column explanation for Table A.6:

(1) Product identity

(2) Batch size from product master file

(3) 80 of each part ÷ column 2 = column 3

(4) Cost of each material movement from Table A.3

(5) Column 3 × column 4 = column 5

(6) Column 5 ÷ 80 of each part = column 6

(7) Product identity

(8) Batch size from product master file

(9) Cost of each setup from Table A.3

(10) Column 8 × column 9 = column 10

(11) Column 10 ÷ 80 of each part = column 11

Now we can determine the product unit fixed cost that is attributable to batch-level drivers.

Table A.7 Summary of Unit Fixed Costs Attributable to Batch-Level Drivers

Product	(a) Unit Cost for Material Handling	(b) Unit Cost for Setup	(c) Unit Cost of Batch-Level Drivers (a) + (b)
Valve body	$1.25	$ .50	$1.75
Axle housing	$6.25	$2.50	$8.75
Differential case	$5.00	$2.00	$7.00
Wheel hub	$3.125	$1.25	$4.375
Brake caliper	$3.125	$1.25	$4.375

Now the total unit fixed cost per product developed via activity-based costing can be summarized.

Table A.8 Determination of Total Fixed Cost per Unit Using ABC

Product	Facility- Level Driver	Product- Line Driver (Table A.5)	Batch-Level Driver (Table A.7)	Total Unit Fixed Cost Using ABC Methods
Valve body	$1.00	$7.50	$1.75	$10.25
Axle housing	$1.00	$6.875	$8.75	$16.625
Differential case	$1.00	$1.875	$7.00	$ 9.875
Wheel hub	$1.00	$7.81	$4.375	$13.185
Brake caliper	$1.00	$7.19	$4.375	$12.565

We have now developed unit fixed costs that have been analytically developed and carried out to three decimal places.

What we need to remember, however, is that all we have done is neatly assigned all of our $5,000 monthly fixed cost to our product mix. The question still remains: If we were to make 79 valve bodies instead of 80 per month, would our total plant's fixed cost be reduced by $10.25 (see Table A.8) to $4,989.75?

The fact remains that fixed costs that exist as a function of time have nothing in common with costs that behave relative to production volume. Why then, treat them as if they did?

APPENDIX B

Using Excel Solver to Execute the OpTek Algorithm

The contents of this appendix will take the reader through detailed step-by-step instructions on how to duplicate the solutions to examples and tables relative to OpTek Corporation in the text. The initial input data as well as the spreadsheet format are found on the enclosed CD-ROM.

Although the initial objective of this appendix is to teach by way of duplication, the ultimate objective is for readers to be able to inject specific data relative to their own operations.

The reader will, therefore, find this appendix to be one continuous exercise on the application of optimization technology.

The Software

Existing spreadsheet software facilitates the execution of the OpTek Algorithm quite handily. The Solver module of Microsoft's Excel is perhaps the most widely used in industry. The Solver module can be found on Microsoft's Office 97 software or software produced later. Corel also has like capabilities found in Quattro Pro under the Numeric Tools, Optimizer module.

Due to the wide popularity of Excel Solver, we will use it to explain and illustrate the working of the OpTek Algorithm. Quattro Pro, however, is very similar to Excel. The functions are very much alike, with only minor differences in terminology.

Formatting the Gross Profit Maximization Problem for the Solver

(As presented in Table 3.1 [p. 27] in main text)

An optimization problem, either in the form of maximization or minimization, begins with an objective. The objective in the present case is to determine the product mix that will result in the highest possible gross profit for the OpTek plant within the capabilities of its production resources.

In light of the above paragraph, the routing of each product must be known, as well as each department's capacity and availability. This information was originally documented in Table 2.4 (p. 16) and is reproduced below for your convenience.

Table B.1 Routing Matrix for OpTek Corporation

Department (Resource)	Valve Body	Axle Housing	Differential Case	Wheel Hub	Brake Caliper	Time Available
Core	.4	.8	.1	.3	.9	200 hrs.
Assembly	.7	.2	.1	.2	.7	200 hrs.
Molding	.5	.5	.5	.5	.5	200 hrs.
Cleaning	.1	.7	.2	.1	.6	200 hrs.
Grinding	.3	.3	.1	.2	.8	200 hrs.

Whatever objective we choose, the answer is *always* subject to the above routings and resource capacities.

Considering that the present objective is gross profit maximization for the OpTek Plant, we also need to know the gross profit for each product.

Table B.2 Gross Profit for Individual Products

Product Description	Gross Profit *(from Table 2.2, p. 14)*
Valve body	$ 5.00
Axle housing	$10.00
Differential case	$ 5.00
Wheel hub	$11.00
Brake caliper	$ 1.50

Now Solver will be able to determine the product mix for the OpTek plant that will provide the highest possible total gross profit.

The initial step is to open a spreadsheet and:

1. Enter product descriptions in cells B2 through F2.
2. Enter department (resource) descriptions in cells A3 through A7.
3. Label cell A8 "gross profit each" and then enter individual product gross profit in cells B8 through F8 from Table B.2.
4. Label cell A9 "number of parts," which will be determined by Solver and reflected in cells B9 through F9.

See Figure B.1.

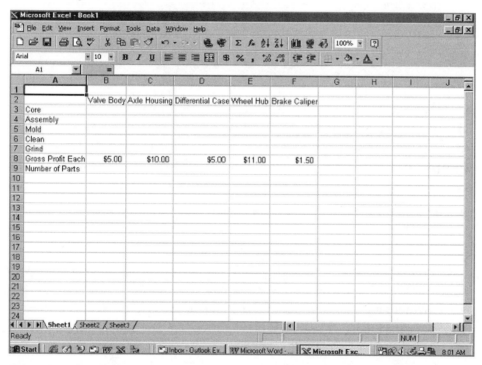

Figure B.1 Spreadsheet Screen Reflecting Items 1 Through 4 Above

The next step is to express the routing matrix, (Table B.1) in cells on our spreadsheet. Each entry in the routing matrix must be multiplied by the number of parts that will be determined by Solver to achieve the objective and subsequently reflected in Row 9. For example:

Cell B3 = the amount of time required to process one valve body through the core process multiplied by the number of valve bodies to pass through the core process as determined when the problem is solved.

Cell B3 = .4 × B9 = .4*B9

Each cell will initially reflect "0" as each equation is entered because the number of each part to be determined by Solver and subsequently entered on row 9 is zero before the problem is solved, and any number multiplied by zero is zero. Therefore, we will illustrate how the matrix would appear as Table B.3.

Table B.3 Representation of Routing Matrix (Table B.1) in Spreadsheet Format

Rows	B	C	D	E	F
3	=.4*B9	=.8*C9	=.1*D9	=.3*E9	=.9*F9
4	=.7*B9	=.2*C9	=.1*D9	=.2*E9	=.7*F9
5	=.5*B9	=.5*C9	=.5*D9	=.5*E9	=.5*F9
6	=.1*B9	=.7*C9	=.2*D9	=.1*E9	=.6*F9
7	=.3*B9	=.3*C9	=.1*D9	=.2*E9	=.8*F9

The next step is to label cell A10, "total gross profit." Solver will then calculate the gross profit generated by each product in cells B10 through F10 as the product mix that maximizes total plant gross profit is determined. For example cell B10 will contain the equation B8 × B9, i.e., =B8*B9 or the individual part gross profit multiplied by the number of each part determined by Solver.

Table B.4 Representation of Gross Profit Determination per Product in Spreadsheet Format

	B	C	D	E	F
10	=B8*B9	=C8*C9	=D8*D9	=E8*E9	=F8*F9

Provisions must now be made for the total hours for each work center, total number of parts produced, and total plant gross profit. For example, label cell G2 "totals" and then enter the following formulas into the cells as illustrated. For example, the procedure is to highlight cell G3. Then click on the Σ symbol on the tool bar. Next, highlight cell B3 and drag your mouse over through cell F3. Enter this formula:

G3 = ΣB3:F3
G4 = ΣB4:F4
G5 = ΣB5:F5
G6 = ΣB6:F6
G7 = ΣB7:F7

There is, of course, no need to summarize the entries in row 8, that is, gross profit per part.

G9 = ΣB9:F9

G10 = ΣB10:F10

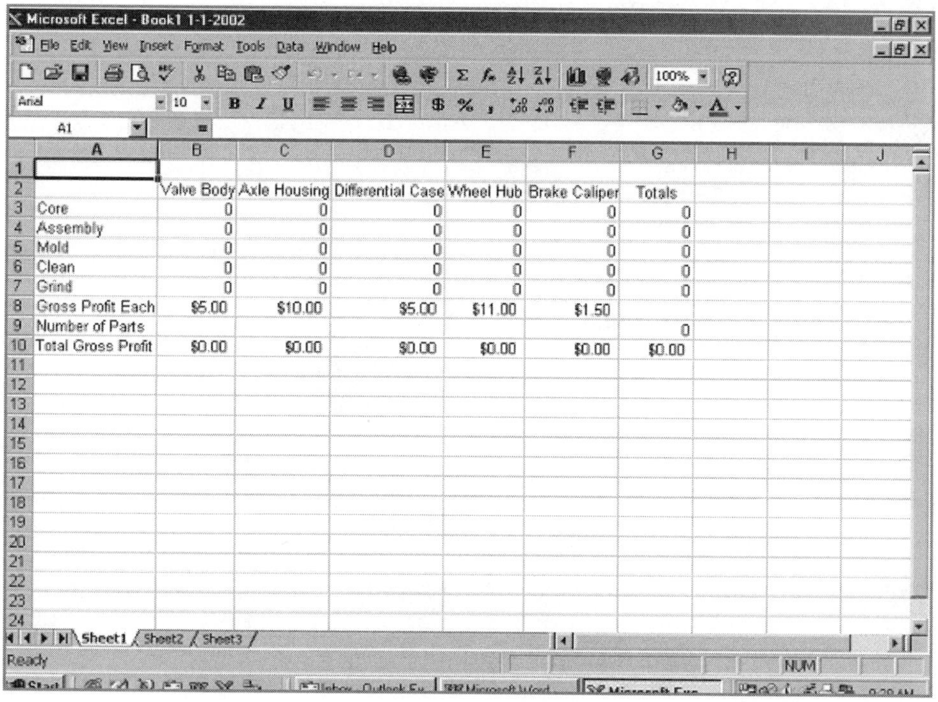

	A	B	C	D	E	F	G
2		Valve Body	Axle Housing	Differential Case	Wheel Hub	Brake Caliper	Totals
3	Core	0	0	0	0	0	0
4	Assembly	0	0	0	0	0	0
5	Mold	0	0	0	0	0	0
6	Clean	0	0	0	0	0	0
7	Grind	0	0	0	0	0	0
8	Gross Profit Each	$5.00	$10.00	$5.00	$11.00	$1.50	
9	Number of Parts						0
10	Total Gross Profit	$0.00	$0.00	$0.00	$0.00	$0.00	$0.00

Figure B.2 Spreadsheet Reflecting Data Set Complete

Using the Solver Module

The majority of work has been done. Now we click on Tools and highlight and select Solver.

Solver will ask for several items of information termed Solver Parameters. The first item of information requested is the "set target cell." The target cell will contain the answer for our problem or objective. Inasmuch as our objective is to maximize gross profit in OpTek's plant, the target cell will be G10, i.e., total gross profit. We simply click on this cell and that cell identification appears in the target cell position on the Solver window.

The next parameter requested by Solver is whether our problem has a maximization or minimization objective. We clearly desire to maximize gross profit and, therefore, will click on the maximization choice.

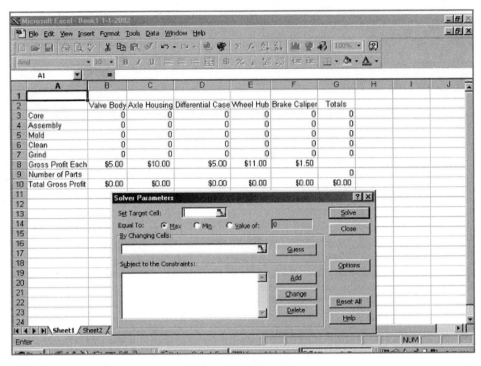

Figure B.3 Spreadsheet Illustrating the Solver Window

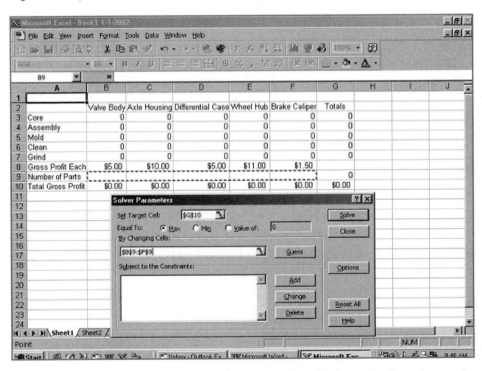

Figure B.4 Spreadsheet Showing Data Set, Target Cell, Optimization Function, and Changing Cells

The next parameter requested is termed "by changing cells." These are the cells whose values are determined by Solver to meet the objective of gross profit maximization. The changing cells in the present example are the numbers of each product required to meet our objective of maximizing total plant gross profit, i.e., cells B9 through F9. We simply highlight the area designated "by changing cells" and drag our mouse across cells B9 through F9.

Next, and last, we must enter any constraints that may limit the amount of gross profit that the OpTek plant can generate. The plant's constraints are the number of hours available per month for each department/resource. The available capacity for each department/resource has been previously noted from Table B.1 as 200 hours for each. We click on the "subject to the constraint" portion of the Solver window and then click on "add." The total department/resource hours are found on our spreadsheet in column G. Therefore, cells G3, G4, G5, G6, and G7 must be =< 200 hours. We insert the constraints one at a time. For example, the procedure is to click on "add" and insert each capacity constraint in the following format:

G3 =< 200 hours

One final note on constraints: We must also insert a non-negativity constraint for our changing cells B9 through F9 because the number of parts cannot be less than zero. The format would be B9:F9 => 0.

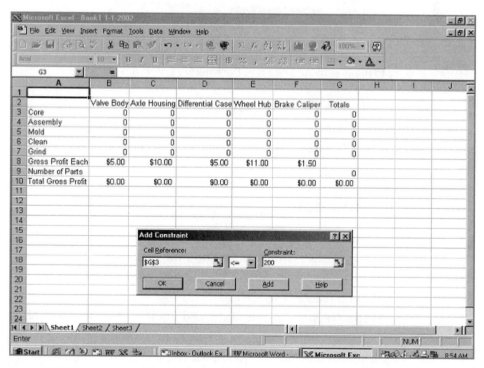

Figure B.5 Illustration of the Addition of Constraints to the Data Set

After all of the constraints are added, we are ready to solve the problem and review the output, i.e., the maximum gross profit that the OpTek plant could generate with existing conditions. The spreadsheet will look like the following after all of the input data has been entered:

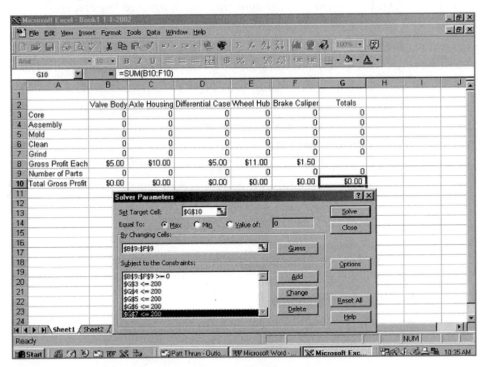

Figure B.6 Spreadsheet with All Data and Parameters Entered

Now we simply click on "solve" and in the twinkling of an eye the answer is found. The maximum gross profit that the OpTek Plant can generate with existing conditions is $4,400. The spreadsheet should now be compared with Table 3.1 (p. 27) in the main text.

Ancillary Information

On the "reports" space in the window in Figure B.7, click on "answer" and review this report. Note that in the "constraint" section the only binding department/resource constraint is cell G-5, molding. This department/resource has used all available 200 hours and reflects zero slack.

Go back to the "reports" space again and click on "sensitivity." Note the "Lagrange multiplier" in the constraints section. The $22 value opposite the molding constraint represents the additional amount of gross profit that the

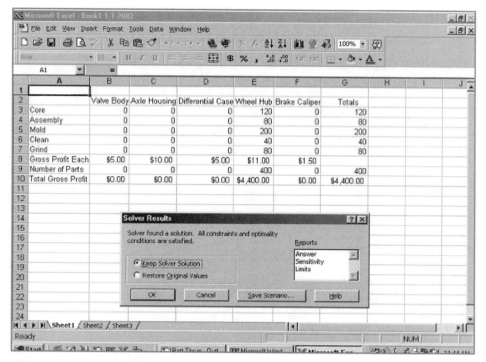

Figure B.7 Solved Problem

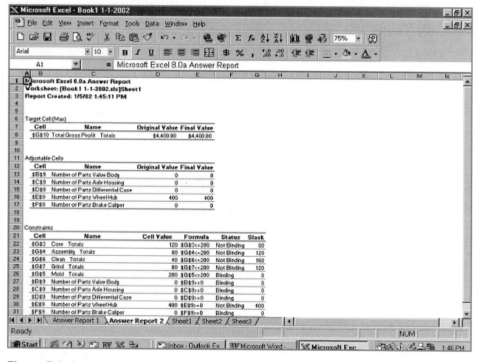

Figure B.8 Accompanying Answer Report Reflecting Molding as the Only Binding Constraint

OpTek plant could generate if the molding constraint were elevated by one constraint unit, that is, the addition of one more hour of capacity.

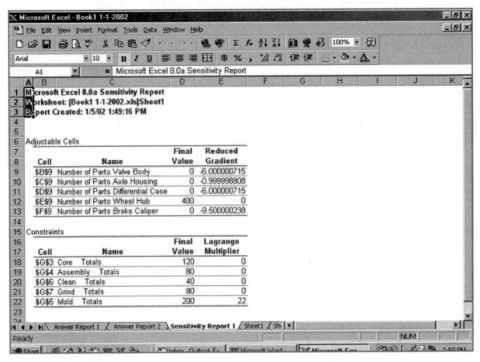

Figure B.9 Lagrange Multiplier Reflecting $22 Opportunity in the Molding Constraint

At this time, go back and review in detail the section entitled "opportunity" p. 28) following Table 3.1 in the main text. Now that we see how to set up and solve an optimization problem with the Solver, further simulation will be relatively simple.

Using the Same Routings and Capacities for Future Simulations

This section of Appendix B should not be read until after completing Chapter 4 in the main text.

After completing Chapter 4, go back to Figure B.7 and close the Solver Results window.

Calculating Contribution Maximization

On Figure B.7, label cell A11 "contribution each" and insert each part's respective contribution from main Table 4.13 (p. 45) into cells B11 through F11.

Next, label cell A12 "total contribution." The formula for cells B12 through F12 will be each part's contribution multiplied by the number of parts each to be determined in row 9 as before.

Example:

Cell B12 = B9*B11, etc.

Remember to include the following formula for total plant contribution in cell G12:

Cell G12 = ΣB12:F12

Once again, we bring Solver down and change the parameters as needed. It is quickly realized that the only parameter that needs to be changed is the identification of the changing cell. It now becomes G12. That is the only change required. Click on "solve" and review the results.

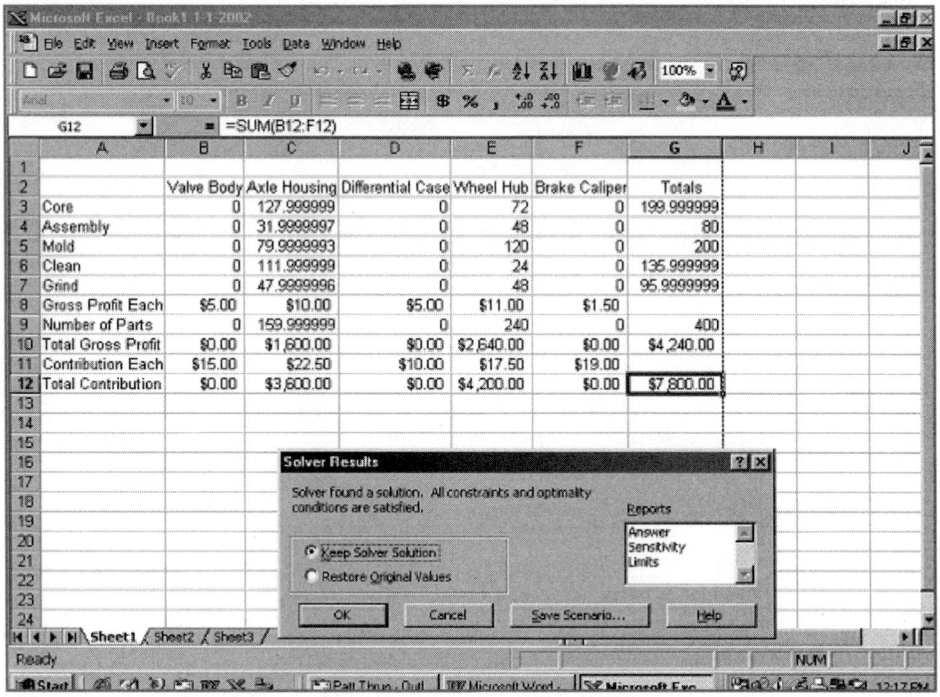

	Valve Body	Axle Housing	Differential Case	Wheel Hub	Brake Caliper	Totals
Core	0	127.999999	0	72	0	199.999999
Assembly	0	31.9999997	0	48	0	80
Mold	0	79.9999993	0	120	0	200
Clean	0	111.999999	0	24	0	135.999999
Grind	0	47.9999996	0	48	0	95.9999999
Gross Profit Each	$5.00	$10.00	$5.00	$11.00	$1.50	
Number of Parts	0	159.999999	0	240	0	400
Total Gross Profit	$0.00	$1,600.00	$0.00	$2,640.00	$0.00	$4,240.00
Contribution Each	$15.00	$22.50	$10.00	$17.50	$19.00	
Total Contribution	$0.00	$3,600.00	$0.00	$4,200.00	$0.00	$7,800.00

Figure B.10 Calculation of OpTek's Maximum Contribution

Notice the new product mix in Row 9. Note also the total plant gross profit of $4,240 in cell G10 when plant contribution is maximized in cell G12.

On Figure B.10, we can insert revenue per part, throughput per part, variable cost per part, process time per part, etc., and solve. We can easily duplicate Table 4.16 (p. 48) in the main text. For example, if we wanted to duplicate line 1 in Table 4.16, *Maximize contribution*, the parameters for revenue, throughput, variable cost, utilization, and contribution must be included on the spreadsheet and the target cell would be "Total contribution." If we wanted to duplicate line 3, that is, *Maximize revenue*, we would simply designate "total revenue" as the target cell. If we wanted to duplicate Line 2, that is, *Minimize variable cost*, we need to also select the *minimization* objective on the Solver Parameters window in addition to designating "total variable cost" as the target cell.

Routings, Capacities, and Contribution

If a plant can express its manufacturing operational improvements in terms of its routings, department available hours, and individual part contributions, then it can accurately measure the financial benefits (bottom-line impact) of such operating improvements.

West Coast Processors: A Case Study

Introducing West Coast Processors

West Coast Processors (WCP) is also a real company; however, WCP is not the real name. The reason for using a fictitious name is because live financial data will be used in this case. We thought it would be beneficial to present a case for a *process* industry using actual data and numbers. The applicability of the concepts to *discrete manufacturing* was illustrated with the OpTek example.

WCP is a manufacturer whose primary production processes are accomplished via continuous flow. Depending on the application, there are additional finishing steps that are all batch processes. WCP had a total of six processes producing 33 products.

In 1990, the plant was losing in excess of $2MM per year and had lost money in the previous eight years. WCP had done what had been considered to be all of the right things.

During the first three years, the plant manager had rigorously worked on improving productivity with equipment improvement, automation, and cost reductions. After these efforts were completed, the plant was earning approximately $2.5MM per year. While this was a significant achievement, this was still not enough to produce an acceptable return on investment. Unfortunately, all of the plant manager's 'big' ideas had been implemented, and WCP was still not as profitable as it needed to be.

It was about this time that a brochure came in the mail describing a seminar entitled "Managing Constraints: It's About Time," and the facilitator was Walt Thrun. This seminar was advertised as introducing methodology that could substantially improve manufacturing profitability. After some investigation, WCP retained him for a two-day seminar to present his concepts. The plant manager admitted that at the end of the seminar he was just a little skeptical. After all, the controller and Cost Accounting Department had spent years developing and refining the budgeting system, and WCP had been using it for years to provide detailed cost analysis and to project profitability. Now, all of a sudden, the seminar implied that there was a new and better way. Even though he was skeptical, the plant manager didn't think too highly of those who attended training and then would go back to "business as usual."

So the necessary data was gathered and a model was built for the plant. The manager found it very interesting that his educational background consisted primarily of a Masters of Science degree in mechanical engineering, and yet the seminar provided all the information for him to develop the model for WCP without a background in finance or accounting.

Existing Planning and Budgeting Methodology

The existing procedure for developing the plant load and mix was very typical and included the following steps:

1. The sales and marketing group would estimate product volumes and provide this information to the production group.
2. The production people would develop the annual budget based on the above sales projections.
3. The accounting people would allocate the plant's fixed cost to the various processes and subsequently to the products.

All those involved were convinced that WCP had to achieve the maximum plant design output of 28MM gallons of product per year to cover the high-fixed-cost allocations. Now the manager was really skeptical. He had employed all of the engineering ingenuity to process improvements and cost reductions, and had invested all of the capital that was feasible to achieve this 28MM gallon design capacity. What else could possibly be done?

The Suggested Methodology and Data Requirements Were Surprisingly Simple

The data requirements to run the model were very basic, so they continued. The following data was all that was required for the initial run:

1. Selling price per item that was already known.
2. Variable cost per product that was already available.

3. Available capacity hours for each process per year.
4. All product process routings expressed in hours per gallon instead of gallons per hour:
   - The process capabilities are expressed in time units, not gallons.
   - The seminar taught that "It's all about time!" (Gallons may vary with product mix, but hours will remain constant.)
5. Knowing items 1 and 2 above, WCP could easily calculate each product's contribution, which was the objective for the algorithm.

Trial Run Using Live Data

The initial trial consisted of eight of the 33 total products chosen at random and all six of the processes. The statistics for the eight products follow:

Table C.1 Selling Prices, Cost, and Profit Statistics for Eight Products for West Coast Processors Used in Initial Optimization Trial

Products	2480	1660	H52	2480+	1660+	40R	500	1680RS
Selling price	.6340	.5998	.7400	.8978	.8844	.3329	1.0300	.4683
Variable cost	.2529	.2475	.3377	.3354	.3285	.1731	.3140	.1772
Allocated fixed cost	.3161	.2627	.2667	.4236	.4096	.2438	.7300	.2279
Gross profit	.0650	.0896	.1356	.1388	.1463	(.0840)	(.0140)	.0632
Contribution	.3811	.3523	.4023	.5624	.5559	.1598	.7160	.2911

The next information needed in order to test the model for WCP was to examine the routings through the plant for the eight products selected for the trial. The relevant routing matrix follows. All routing times are expressed in hours per gallon of product.

Table C.2 Routing Matrix for West Coast Processors

Products	2480	1660	H52	2480+	1660+	40R	500	1680RS
Wash	.000346	.000288	.000297	.000336	.000318	0	.000346	0
Separate	0	0	0	.000864	.000864	0	0	0
Mix	0	0	0	0	0	.00068	0	.000654
Homogenize	0	0	0	0	0	0	0	0
Test	0	0	0	0	0	.000714	0	0
Fill	0	0	0	0	0	0	.003003	0

The final entry to the data set was the recognition of the work-center capacities. They are expressed as hours per year of available time.

Table C.3 Recognition of Plant Capacity and/or Availability

Work Center	Hours of Runtime Available per Year
Wash	8,177 hrs.
Separate	6,149 hrs.
Mix	6,955 hrs.
Homogenize	6,149 hrs.
Test	6,149 hrs.
Fill	4,392 hrs.

At this stage it was time to establish the objective of contribution maximization:

Maximize $.3811 (product 2480) + $.3523 (product 1660) + $.4023 (product H52) + $.5624 (product 2480+) + $.5559 (product 1660+) + $.1598 (product 40R) + $.7160 (product 500) + $.2911 (product 1680RS)

(Subject to the product routings and work-center capacities in Tables C.2 and C.3.)

The contribution maximizing product mix is found below in Table C.4.

Table C.4 Contribution Maximizing Product Mix for West Coast Processors Using the Eight-Product Trial Run

Objective: **Maximize Contribution**

Product	Qty.	Work Center	Hrs. Required	Slack	Opportunity
2480	0	Wash	8,177	0	1,354.55
1660	0	Separate	6,149	0	144.85
H52	18,208,042	Mix	6,955	0	455.11
2480+	0	Homogenize	0	6,149	0
1660+	7,116,898	Test	0	6,149	0
40R	0	Fill	4,392	0	82.36
500	1,462,537				
1680RS	10,634,557				
Total	37,422,034				
Maximum contribution possible $15,424,273					

This initial test absolutely convinced the plant manager to rerun the model with all 33 products. The very first product listed on Table C.4, 2480, did not even show up in the optimum product mix; however, they were presently allocating over one-third of the annual capacity to this product.

Preparing to Run the Model with All 33 Products and Six Work Centers

Please note that the operating profit for the plant for the current year was budgeted at $2.6MM.

They ran the model for the first time with all 33 products and all work centers with contribution maximization as the objective and the results were astounding. The projected operating profit was $16MM per year! The model results pointed out several other very interesting and surprising things:

1. The model stated that WCP should shut down three of the finishing processes.
2. According to the model, the plant should use its capacity to make a product known as 1220. The ironic thing about this recommendation was that the plant manager had fought a long hard battle to keep this product out of the plant because this was the slowest-running product in the plant. If the company ran any of this product it could never achieve the objective design capacity of 28MM gallons of product per year.

    The model clearly showed, however, that the operating profit of $16MM per year could be generated (remember, the budgeted profit was $2.6MM), while producing 16MM gallons instead of the design capacity of 28MM gallons.
3. The model also suggested that the product known as 2480 was the least desirable from a profitability standpoint. This was also totally different from present thinking because the present product mix consisted of more than 35 percent of this product in the current annual plan.

The Manager's Original Skepticism Was Quickly Turning to Cautious Optimism

Inasmuch as the model had indicated that 1220 would provide the most plant profit, the manager contacted the marketing people to get them to tell him how much of this product the market would support. He felt that the model-recommended volume of 16MM gallons wasn't feasible. Sure enough, they told him that the estimated market at existing prices was only approximately 1.5MM gallons per year. So the first marketing constraint was added to the model, that is, limiting the production of 1220 to <= 1.5MM gallons.

Using the Model Was an Iterative Process

The model was run again, and new products would emerge in the recommended optimum product mix. After each iteration, the manager would check with the marketing people to get their input as to their ability to sell the recommended mix. Finally, the model generated a product mix that was realistic from a marketing standpoint.

There were several very interesting things about the mix and the resulting financial impact:

1. The optimum (profit maximizing) product mix indicated that the plant was ideally suited to make a product known as 1660 that, heretofore, had not been considered a desirable product.
2. The plant had currently been making between 35 percent and 40 percent of a product known as 2480. This product was not even found in the final optimum product mix.
3. Many times in the past, WCP had considered shutting down one of the finishing process steps because the fixed cost allocation indicated that this was an unprofitable operation. The model indicated, however, that this finishing step contributed to making the product known as 1660, which was revealed by the model to be included in the most profitable product mix of the plant in total.
4. Conversely, WCP had recently installed a new finishing batch process at a capital investment of approximately $1MM. The model revealed that there was no requirement for this process in the optimum product mix. The ending result was that WCP had made an unwise investment decision.
5. The final model-generated product mix provided an operating profit of slightly more than $6MM, which was 231 percent more than the planned profit using traditional planning methods.
6. Finally, the profit optimizing product mix consisted of just 24MM gallons, or 4MM gallons less than the previously determined plant capacity of 28MM gallons. In essence, the plant would generate 231 percent more profit utilizing just 86 percent of the existing design capacity.

Original Objection from the Marketing and Finance Departments

The newly determined plant capacity of 24MM gallons versus the traditionally determined capacity of 28MM gallons was the initial stumbling block for the marketing and financial people. They contended that the plant should not begin to turn down business until the 28MM-gallon design plant capacity was reached. The model made it apparent that WCP did not need to turn away business in order to make the transition from the current product mix to the more profitable mix suggested by the model. In fact, current sales volumes exceeded the model-generated volume. Their objective was refuted via the pricing mechanism. One of the model outputs was the price sensitivity of each product. The plant could see how much a product's price could be lowered in order to keep it in the optimum mix or how much a product's price would need to be increased in order to bring it in to the optimum mix without compromising the total projected plant contribution. The marketing people could then begin to adjust prices in order to align current product sales volumes with the product mix and volumes provided by the model.

At the next annual plant manager's meeting, WCP's manager presented the final results of the model. The author spent several hours presenting the overall concepts of the model to the plant managers and CEO, and WCP's manager followed up with a presentation of the application of the model for his specific plant using products and pricing suggested and espoused by WCP's own marketing and financial people.

The concepts were embraced in total. The vice president of WCP was instructed to develop a plan for the implementation of the model in domestic operations.

Other Benefits Provided by Using the Model

Two-tier pricing opportunity

The model was extremely easy to use for simulation purposes. For example, during the testing of the model, the plant manager was asked for his opinion as to whether or not WCP should take on some low-priced 2480. The model quickly accommodated this two-tier pricing challenge. He simply added the lower priced 2480 as an individual product and ran the model to determine the financial impact.

Within an hour, he had a reliable, justifiable answer rather than an educated guess. The resulting answer measured the result of the proposal expressed in incremental plant contribution. Had the question been given to the cost accounting people, the answer would have required several hours of analysis that would have provided a distorted answer at best.

Capital Project Analysis and Budgeting

As mentioned earlier, if WCP had used this model last year, it could have avoided the $1MM investment in the new finishing process.

Furthermore, by using the model now, the production constraints were readily identified. Not only that, the financial benefits of relieving them were easily determined. In this case, the plant's predominant constraint with the newly defined optimum product mix was one of the finishing processes (the one that WCP had previously considered shutting down). WCP simply determined the total plant contribution generated from the optimum product mix with existing capacity. Then WCP examined the proposed total plant contribution when capacity was added to this finishing process constraint. The difference in total plant contribution was the cash flow, or financial benefit of adding finishing process capacity.

The financial benefit or cash flow, allowed WCP to compare the projected benefits of having this additional capacity with the required investment for the equipment.

Summary Statement

These new methods represented the most valuable tool for managing a manufacturing operation that WCP's manager had encountered in his postschool days.

WCP's manager had learned several specific points that are universally applicable to users of optimization techniques:

- Making effective operational improvements do not translate to financial advantage.
- WCP's plant did not need to operate at full capacity in order to maximize its profit potential.
- Overhead allocation to products based on labor content leads to incorrect assumptions relative to product desirability.
- Individual product price/cost relationships have nothing to do with total plant profitability.
- Allowing the marketing team to establish market constraints gave WCP ownership in the overall financial results.
- Optimization techniques can eliminate unwise capital investment decisions.

APPENDIX D

Other Proponents and Applications of Optimization Techniques

Applications of optimization techniques have been around for several decades, but the application of such techniques relative to strategic and aggregate planning for manufacturers is just coming of age.

This appendix will cite and briefly expand on the accomplishments of four excellent sources that present optimization techniques relative to manufacturing planning activities.

Note: While optimization techniques include both linear and nonlinear problems, the sources below have chosen to present their applications in the linear format using linear programming.

1. Wallace J. Hopp and Mark L. Spearman, *Factory Physics: Foundations of Manufacturing Management*. Richard D. Irwin, 1996.

    The scope of this very credible work is the operational aspects of an enterprise, that is, the application of resources to the production of goods and services. A narrower focus is directed toward manufacturing activities, hence the book concerns manufacturing management.

    Readers will learn how to apply moderately rigorous quantitative tools to achieve the fundamental objective of a manufacturing firm stated as "to increase the well-being of its stakeholders by making a good return on investment over the long term."

    In addition, the authors presented their case that the achievement of the above objective could best be done with optimization models that transcend traditional static standard cost methods and intuition. The quotation below is found in Chapter 6 of their book entitled **"Objectives, Measures, and Control"** (p. 209):

> *A static cost-based model, no matter how detailed, cannot accurately assign costs to limited resources, such as machines subject to capacity constraints, and therefore may produce misleading results. Only a more sophisticated optimization model, which dynamically determines the costs of such resources as it computes the optimal plan, can be guaranteed to avoid this.*
>
> *In addition to offering an alternative to the cost-accounting perspective, constrained optimization models are useful in a wide variety of operations management problems.*

Another application of optimization models found in *Factory Physics* pertains to the aggregate planning process. Aggregate planning addresses the level of resources required to support a suggested production plan for the time period approximating one year.

Part III is entitled **"Principles in Practice,"** and Chapter 16, contained in Part III, is entitled **"Aggregate and Workforce Planning."** This quote from the chapter is found on pages 502–503:

> *A variety of manufacturing management decisions require information about what a plant will produce over the next year or two. The module in which we address the important question of what will be produced and when it will be produced over the long range is the aggregate planning module. The aggregate planning module occupies a central position in the production planning and control hierarchy. The reason, of course, is that so many important decisions . . . depend on a long-term production plan.*
>
> *As we mentioned, linear programming is a particularly useful tool for formulating and solving many of the problems commonly faced in the aggregate planning and workforce planning modules.*
>
> *No trick that chooses a dominant product or identifies the bottleneck before knowing the product mix can find the optimal solution in general. While such tricks can work for specific problems, they can result in extremely bad solutions in others. The only method guaranteed to solve these problems optimally is an exact algorithm such as those used in linear programming packages.*

The authors then include a section in this chapter entitled "Using the Excel LP Solver."

2. Richard B. Chase, Nicholas J. Aquilano, and F. Robert Jacobs, *Operations Management for Competitive Advantage*, 9th ed. McGraw-Hill/Irwin, 2001.

This book is targeted primarily for the academic audience and is used for an introductory course in **production and operations management**. Such a course is part of the basic core curriculum for many business schools.

The authors state that the goal of operations management is to: "efficiently create wealth by supplying quality goods and services."

They further state that their objective for the current book is to cover the latest and the most important issues facing operations managers, as well as the basic tools and techniques.

Section 4 of the text is entitled "Planning and Controlling the Supply Chain." Included in the section is Chapter 12, entitled "Aggregate Planning."

These authors also consider the aggregate plan to be a broad plan listing output and resources required to produce that output for the planning period of approximately one year. They state that the objective of the aggregate plan is to minimize the cost of resources required to meet demand over the planning period. Specific quotations from this book include:

The general model of linear programming is appropriate to aggregate planning if the cost and variable relationships are linear and demand can be treated as deterministic.

Regarding application of sophisticated aggregate planning techniques in industry, only linear programming has seen wide usage. Much of this is being done using the Solver Option in Microsoft Excel ....

The text then includes a separate supplement entitled "Linear Programming with the Excel Solver."

3. Norman Gaither and Greg Frazier, *Production and Operations Management*, 8th ed. South-Western College Publishing, 1999.

This book is also addressed primarily to college students. It is used at both undergraduate and graduate levels. It presents **production and operations management** as the integrating piece of the puzzle that allows all the functional areas of an organization to work together.

This excellent text refers to optimization techniques in the form of linear programming relative to production/operations management in four separate chapters:

The authors present the initial application of linear programming for the product mix challenge when the single objective is to maximize profit (p. 198): "To select the mix of products or services that results in maximum profits for the planning period."

This text also presents a lengthy appendix entitled "Linear Programming Solution Methods."

The appendix to the book focuses more on methodology than computer software. Just as we did with OpTek in this book, this initial focus was developing the algorithm to solve the optimization problem. We then presented the Excel Solver as a means to execute the algorithm.

4. Don R. Hansen and Maryanne M. Mowen, *Management Accounting*, 5th ed. South-Western College Publishing, 2000.

As the title implies, this is a management accounting text. The term *management accounting* has been used to designate the movement forward from the more traditional *cost accounting*. This text, along with the others addressing the discipline, has much more coverage of what has been termed "activity-based management" or "activity-based costing."

Although activity-based management is an improvement over the more traditional standard cost accounting methodology, it still attempts to assign fixed periodic costs to units of production. It is really an example of trying to do the wrong thing better. As such, activity-based costing has little if nothing to do with optimization technology.

However, there is a bright spot with some of the newer management accounting texts: this one introduces the concept of optimization techniques.

Part III of this text is entitled "Management Decision Making." Chapter 17 of this section is entitled "Tactical Decision Making."

The following quotation is found on page 708:

The linear programming model is an important tool for making product mix decisions, though it requires very little independent managerial decision making. The mix decision is made by the linear programming model itself. Assuming that the linear programming model is a reasonable representation of reality, the main role for management is to ensure that accurate data are used as input to the model. This includes the ability to recognize the irrelevance of fixed costs and the ability to assess the accounting and technological inputs accurately (for example, the unit selling prices, the unit costs, and the amount of resource consumed by each product as it is produced.)

Note: It is encouraging to see the quotation above included in a management accounting text. Although rather short, it is a good inclusion, considering that the remainder of this text and the other leading managerial texts are filled from cover to cover with teaching students what we have termed counterproductive practices.

Glossary of Terms

Activity-Based Costing (ABC)

A multistep overhead assignment process whereby costs are initially assigned, or charged, to activities that consume resources, and then subsequently assigned to the products that utilize those activities.

Aggregate Plan

The firm's overall production and accompanying resource requirements plan expressed in generic units of production, or units of capacity, usually representing a planning horizon approximating a year.

Asset

The monetary value of a production factor awaiting consumption in the production process and represented on the firm's balance sheet.

Balance Sheet

A static representation of a firm's financial position as of a given point on the unending time span. This primary financial statement lists the monetary value of all of the firm's production factors as well as the ownership status of such assets, i.e., liabilities to others or equity for the owners.

Batch-Level Driver

This term is used in conjunction with *activity-based costing*. A batch-level driver is the level of a given activity that benefits a batch of products, such as a container of the same product moved to another location. That movement benefits each unit of product in that container equally.

Benchmark Product Mix

The product mix that provides maximum total plant contribution within the confines of that plant's product routings and resource capacities. This term can be used interchangeably with *optimum product mix*. Once this product mix is determined, it is used as the benchmark to measure the financial impact of any proposed manufacturing activity.

Break-Even

The level of utilization of a firm's primary constraint where the value of the revenue exactly equals the value of the resources consumed to generate that revenue. It is represented in equation form as: total revenue minus total variable and fixed costs for a given time period.

Capacity

The level of availability of a given resource, typically expressed in time units for a given time period, for example, the capacity of the molding machine was 200 hours per month. Alternately, the number of units of production that can be produced in a defined time period, for example, the number of molds that could be produced per month was 400.

Capital Budget

A financial plan for the acquisition of depreciable assets to be used to facilitate the production process for a given time period.

Constraint

A factor that limits the amount of a given objective that can be attained. In this book, the primary objective was total plant contribution, and the two primary categories of constraints that limited the amount of contribution were production capacity and market demand.

Constraint Elevation

Relieving a production constraint by means of providing more capacity of the constrained resource.

Constraint Exploitation

The management of all production resources in such a manner as to attain the maximum amount of an objective within the confines of existing conditions.

Contribution

Selling price less variable cost for an individual product. Total revenue less total variable cost for a given time period for a total plant.

Counterproductive Practices

Practices generally associated with performance measures that, if employed, inhibit and, in fact, actually prevent a firm from achieving its profit potential. In this book, this term is used interchangeably with the seven deadly sins of manufacturing.

Cycle Time

The time required to perform a specific operation on a machine-controlled/paced process.

Financial Impact

The monetary effect of a given action expressed in the present context as a change in the amount of total monthly plant contribution.

Fixed Cost

A periodic expense, i.e., the consumption of an asset that is a function of time with no relationship to production activity or levels.

Gross Profit

Selling price less total standard cost (variable cost plus allocated fixed cost) for a given product. Total revenue less total standard cost of sales for a given time period for a total plant.

Idle Capacity

The amount of a nonconstrained resource not required in a given time period. Idle capacity can be expressed for an individual resource or for the total plant. This term is used interchangeably with *slack*.

Income Statement

A primary financial statement that summarizes the net effect of total revenue received compared with the level of resource consumption for a given period of time. The net effect, or "bottom line," is the amount by which a firm's asset base grew for that time period.

Internal Contribution

The total amount of contribution (revenue less variable costs) generated by a plant for a given time period via internal operations without regard to outsourcing activities, etc.

Internal Rate of Return (IRR)

The ratio of incremental contribution provided by a capital proposal compared with the incremental investment required for the proposal. In financial terms, it is the discount rate applied to present and future cash flows associated with a given proposal that brings the net present value of the proposal to zero.

Isolation

A decision made or an action taken with a narrow or focused emphasis without regard to the effects that the decision or action may have on the whole.

Integrative Reasoning

A decision-making process that considers the effects of all relevant factors simultaneously. This type of reasoning can only be accomplished with some type of algorithm.

Lean Manufacturing

A process whereby waste in the form of non-value-added activities are identified and eliminated from the production segment of the value chain.

Market Constraint

The limitation of an objective imposed by the lack of market demand for products.

Multiplant Operations

An environment in which the operations of multiple plants within a corporation are synthesized, resulting in financial optimization of the total corporation vs. the financial optimization of the individual plants.

Net Operating Profit

The profit generated for a defined period resulting exclusively from a plant's primary activities, i.e., the production and sale of products.

Nondiscounted Rate of Return

The ratio of the financial benefits provided by a capital proposal compared with the investment cost of the proposal without regard to the time value of money relative to future cash flows.

Nonstandard Process

An alternate method to perform a given operation that consumes more resources than the preferred, or standard, process. The use of a nonstandard process results in a manufacturing variance.

Objective

Within the context of this book, this term relates to optimization technology and is the expression of what it is that we want to optimize. For example, the objective may be to minimize cost or it may be to maximize revenue.

Opportunity

Within the context of this book, this term relates to optimization technology and represents the incremental value of a specific objective that could be achieved when a constrained resource is elevated by one constraint unit.

OpTek Algorithm

An optimization technique based on linear programming logic developed and used by the Foundry Products Division of the J. I. Case Company in the 1980s.

Optimization Technique

The decision process leading to the one best result for a given objective within a constrained environment. Optimization may be either maximization or minimization, depending on the specific objective involved.

Optimum Product Mix

The product mix resulting when a given objective is met using optimization technology. See *benchmark product mix*.

Outsourcing

The activity resulting from the make-or-buy decision when optimization technology determines that a given product should be purchased from a vendor instead of being manufactured in-house.

Overhead

Necessary manufacturing-related costs required to support the production process but incurred as a function of time and not production activity levels. See *fixed cost.*

Overhead Absorption

An accounting process in which overhead costs are removed from departmental expenditures and transferred to the balance sheet as assets in the form of work-in-process inventory. This accounting process incorrectly implies that such overhead costs actually add value to the partially completed products as they progress through the production process.

Overhead Allocation/Assignment

An accounting process in which fixed costs are allocated, or assigned, arbitrarily to individual products. This arbitrary process incorrectly implies that time period costs can be accurately expressed as unit-driven costs.

Overhead Rate

The amount of overhead allocated or assigned to a given product based on some other activity, i.e., direct labor, for example, for traditional standard cost systems. See *activity-based costing*.

Plant-Level Driver

This term is used in conjunction with *activity-based costing*. A plant level driver is the level of a given activity that benefits all products made in a given plant, such as the leasing of ventilating and air cleaning equipment.

Political Expediency

An action taken without regard to the firm's financial benefit, but rather to enhance one's perceived power position in an organization.

Preventive Maintenance (PM)

Proactive measures to ensure maximum availability of production equipment. Such measures could include the replacement of components of the equipment during scheduled downtime to prevent equipment failure during the production process.

Process Improvements

Changes in product design, equipment, or tooling that result in variable cost reductions, decreased process times, alternate routings, etc., producing an increase in total plant contribution per time period.

Product-Line Driver

This term is used in conjunction with *activity-based costing*. A product-line driver is the level of a given activity that benefits all products in a given product line such as ultrasonic tests. Only the product lines that require such tests will bear the cost of the ultrasonic testing activity.

Product Routing

The processing sequence and rate of resource consumption for each product as it passes through the production process.

Productivity of Capital

The ratio of output divided by input. The productivity of capital considers the input to be the assets of the firm at the beginning of a time period and the output to be the assets at the end of that same period.

Replacement Equipment

Within the context of the capital budgeting process will be found the category of replacement equipment. Such equipment does not elevate a constraint or add capacity but rather replaces old or less-efficient equipment.

Return on Investment (ROI)

The ratio expressed as a percent of the amount of net operating profit achieved compared with the level of assets required to generate that amount of profit for given time period, normally a year. This percent is the same as the *productivity of capital* minus 1.

Revenue

The total amount of money received from the sale of products for a given time period.

Routing Matrix

An extremely significant part of a plant's database. The routing matrix is typically in the form of a table that lists each product in columns and each resource (work center) in rows. At the intersection of each row and column is found the amount of that resource consumed by each product as it passes through that resource. At the end of each row is found the amount of that resource available per time period, and at the end of each column will be found the number of each product determined by optimization technology depending on the specific objective.

Seamless

A process by which the steps define a continuum instead of a series of discrete segments.

Slack

The amount of a nonconstrained resource not required in a given time period. Slack can be expressed for an individual resource or for the total plant. This term is used interchangeably with *idle capacity*.

Standard Cost

A benchmark of what a product should cost under normal conditions. The standard cost of a product using a standard costing system includes not only the standard (expected) cost of the variable components, i.e., direct labor and materials, but also a predetermined portion of the plant's manufacturing overhead. This is the cost at which the product is held in inventory and the subsequent cost of sales when the product is sold.

Subcontractor

In the context of this book, a subcontractor is one who performs a portion of the manufacturing process to be differentiated from the outsourcing process, where the product itself is purchased from an external vendor.

Synergy

A phenomenon that occurs when the overall results are more than the sum of the parts. In the context of this book, synergy occurs when multiple process improvements are made simultaneously, and when more than one constraint is elevated simultaneously.

Throughput

Total revenue less the material cost of goods sold for a given period of time.

Traditional Wisdom/Thinking

The wisdom associated with managing a plant with a standard cost system. Such wisdom includes the thinking that the financial well-being of the total plant will be enhanced by the sum of all individual operational improvements. Such wisdom also includes the notion that the total cost to operate a manufacturing entity can accurately be assigned to individual products.

Unabsorbed Overhead

That amount of overhead expense incurred but not transferred to inventory as an asset. Unabsorbed overhead is reflected as an expense on the income statement in the period incurred. It is typically known also as idle capacity variance. See also *overhead absorption*.

Utilization

The percent of time that a resource is used in relation to the total time it is available for use. Utilization applies to individual resources as well as to the plant in total.

Variable Cost

The cost of manufacturing that is directly proportional to the number of units produced. The primary variable product costs are direct materials and direct labor. Such costs are readily identifiable with a specific unit of production.

Variable Costing Income Statement

In the context of this book, a variable-costing income statement is more narrowly defined as an income statement that does not include overhead allocations. Such a definition excludes the calculation of gross profit. Total fixed overhead for a given period is deducted in total from the contribution generated for the period to arrive at the net operating profit. Subsequently, there is no provision for absorbed or unabsorbed overhead. For operating purposes, overhead is not inventoried and is addressed as it occurs. The net operating profit will be the same when using a variable-costing income statement or the traditional income statement using full-product costing methods.

Variance

The difference between a product's standard cost and that product's actual cost is termed its variance. This term is also applied to unabsorbed overhead, as well as to any part of the manufacturing process where a predetermined standard can be compared with the actual cost of that process.

Index

Excel Solver, 193–204, 214
Exploitation of constraints, 125, 134, 135, 137
External market factors, 117, 118–119, 212, 124

Facility utilization *see also* Plant utilization
   Seven Deadly Sins and, 5
Factory Physics: Foundations of
   Manufacturing Management, 213–214
Financial *see also* Financial impact, Preventive
   Maintenance, Process Improvements
   benefits, 97, 112, 140–142, 143–144
   department objection, 211
   maximum performance, 176
   progress, 113–114
Financial impact
   lost business, of, 73, 74–75
   nonstandard processes, of, 148–149
   replacement equipment, of, 150–151
Financial Performance
   measuring improvement, 48–50, 180
   operating improvements and, 135, 212
   primary financial measures, 155
Fixed benchmark
   time as, 8
Fixed cost per unit, 184
Fixed costs *see* Fixed overhead, Unit fixed cost
Fixed overhead *see also* Overhead
   annual, 112
   applying to product lines, 14
   level of production and, 188
   not allocating to products, 23
   per unit, 22
   product–line drivers and, 190–192
   shifting to different product lines, 22
Forecasting, 117, 118–119, 133
Frazier, Greg, 215

Gaither, Norman, 215
Grinding machine, 140
Gross profit
   low costs and, 41
   maximizing, 26–28, 31, 49
   net operating profit and, 25, 28–32
   optimization technology and, 184
   plant utilization and, 30
Gross profit margins
   Seven Deadly Sins and, 5

Hansen, Don R., 216
Holistic outsourcing decisions, 63, 66–68
Hopp, Wallace J., 213

Idle capacity
   equipment utilization and, 103
   constraints and, 171–172
   idle inventory and, 32
   non–constrained work centers and,
     182–183
   old equipment and, 157
   process changes and, 100
   production constraints and, 54
   subcontracting, and, 83
Idle capacity variance, 18, 28, 31–32, 184
Idle inventory, 32
Income statement *see* Monthly income
   statement
Incorrect assumptions *see also* Intuition,
Isolated thinking, Traditional thinking
   174–176
Incremental contribution, 54, 112, 140
Individual Departmental Overhead Rates *see*
   Departmental Overhead Rates
Individual part contributions
   determination of, 76
   increased, 152
   price increases and, 119–120
   reduced process times and, 141
   total plant contribution and, 89
   total plant profitability and, 80
Individual plant performance, 165, 167,
   168–171
Ineffective practices, 5
Internal manufacturing strengths, 117,
   118–119, 124
Internal rate of return (IRR), 110, 182
Institute of Management Accountants, 6
Integrative reasoning, 58–60
Interdisciplinary teaming, 179, 183
Intuition *see also* Assumptions, Isolated
   thinking, Traditional thinking
   97, 104–105, 176
Inventory
   excess, 83
   valuation, 31
Investment opportunity
   incremental contribution and, 175
   operational benefits and, 151–155
   relieving constraints and, 110
   total plant ROI and, 111–112
IRR, 110, 182
Isolated thinking *see also* Assumptions,
   Intuition, Traditional thinking
   capital projects and, 98
   cash flow and, 103